CAREERS IN FILM AND TELEVISION

So You Want to Be a Film or TV Screenwriter?

Amy Dunkleberger

Enslow Publishers, Inc.
40 Industrial Road
Box 398
Berkeley Heights, NJ 07922
USA

http://www.enslow.com

Library of Congress Cataloging-in-Publication Data

Dunkleberger, Amy.
    So you want to be a film or TV screenwriter? / Amy Dunkleberger. — 1st ed.
        p. cm. — (Careers in film and television)
    Includes bibliographical references and index.
    ISBN-13: 978-0-7660-2645-2
    ISBN-10: 0-7660-2645-0
    1. Motion picture authorship—Vocational guidance—Juvenile literature. 2. Television
    authorship—Vocational guidance—Juvenile literature. I. Title. II. Series.
 PN1996.D845 2007
 808.2'3023—dc22

                                                              2006009732

Printed in the United States of America

10 9 8 7 6 5 4 3 2

CONTENTS

INTRODUCTION

At any given moment on any given day, someone is watching a moving image somewhere. Whether in their neighborhood theaters or in the comfort of their own home, people love to watch movies. According to recent surveys, watching TV and DVDs is America's favorite leisure activity. Movies and TV are true mass media. They appeal to all ages and types, especially young people. Ninety percent of America's teens report going to the movies at least occasionally, and over sixty percent say they watch a DVD at least once a week.

The impact of movies and television on our lives is profound. Like books, magazines, newspapers, and the Internet, moving images influence the way we think and feel about the world. We use them to explain events and define attitudes. They are our favorite points-of-reference.

Novelist Jill Robinson, the daughter of movie producer Dore Schary, once described film's effect on her early life this way: "The movies were my textbooks for everything else in the world. . . . If I saw a college, I would see only cheerleaders or blonds. If I saw New York City, I would want to go to the slums I'd seen in the movies, where the tough kids played. If I went to Chicago, I'd want to see the brawling factories and the gangsters."[1]

The process of script writing involves many steps, but it usually begins with a writer sitting down at his or her computer to record ideas.

As television and movie markets expand, so does the need for talented filmmakers. No other art form employs as broad a range of skills as moviemaking does—everything from actors to art directors, writers to wardrobe supervisors. Films require great technical know-how as well as creative expertise. The end product of all these jobs, of course, is a single, cohesive work.

Learning to "read" and analyze a movie is the first step to creating it. To read a film, the viewer must know how the major components—script, direction, photography, editing, etc.—function and how they are combined to make a movie.

This first book in the *Careers in Film and Television* series focuses on the art of screenwriting, the foundation of contemporary filmmaking. The process of screenwriting involves many steps, from idea to final draft. While the earliest films, called "actualities," had no narrative, moviemakers soon figured out that pieces of film could be put together to tell a story. The very first of these simple film stories were devised by the movie's director, who often shot and edited the picture as well.

The screenwriter (or scenarist as they used to be called) first appeared around 1908. Jeannie Macpherson and Frank E. Woods, who cowrote *The Birth of a Nation* with legendary director D. W. Griffith in 1915, are probably the best-known of the early screenwriters. Until the late 1920s, films were silent, with only a few title cards to establish a setting or

supply a line of dialogue. Scenarists not only had to know how to tell a story entirely through pictures, they also had to know what type of story would make a good moving picture.

With the invention of movie sound, screenwriters began to put words into the mouths of actors. Most early "talkies" were just that—talky. Once the novelty of sound wore off, however, film returned to its visual roots, and screenwriters learned to blend dialogue with action. With that, the modern screenplay, that unique expression of pictures and sound, was born.

ELEMENTS OF SCREENWRITING:
PREMISE, SENSORY STYLE, AND STRUCTURE

In a recent interview, Oscar-winning screenwriter Bo Goldman (*One Flew Over the Cuckoo's Nest*, *Meet Joe Black*) defined his work this way: "Sometimes someone'll ask me what I do, and I say I'm a screenwriter, and he'll say, 'Yeah, I know, but what do you write? The words?' I say, 'Yeah, I do that.' Then he'll say, 'What about what comes next?' So I say, 'Yeah, that too.'"[1]

Just as a homebuilder needs a blueprint to construct a house, a filmmaker needs a screenplay, or literary blueprint, to make a movie. Regardless of what happens during and after shooting, a movie's screenplay guides and inspires filmmakers until the final edit.

As Goldman's statement suggests, screenwriting is an often misunderstood, underrated job. Since the earliest days of motion pictures, however, screenplays have been the key element of filmmaking.

Although movies are a visual medium, and directors and actors receive most of the credit for their outcome, film production always begins with words on a page. Many viewers would be surprised to learn how many moments of their favorite films and television shows are described in detail in their scripts.

Screenwriting is a challenging task. The script must not only convey what will happen in a given story, and to whom, but convey it in a way that suggests a visual interpretation. Using only written text, a screenwriter must think in dramatic as well as photographic terms.

THE PREMISE

Typically, a screenwriter must go through many drafts of a script before a final draft, or shooting script, is completed. Like a game of chess, screenplays are carefully and precisely thought out. Before sitting down to write the first page of the first draft, a screenwriters usually asks a series of questions about the story and sketches out an outline of the plot.

Though it may seem obvious and simple, the most important question a writer asks about a story is, "What is it about?" Specifically, a writer examines the story's premise—its underlying dramatic idea.

In a classically constructed, original screenplay, the premise is the driving force behind every event, every plot development, in the story. In his book *The Art of Dramatic Writing*, twentieth-century dramatist Lajos Egri defines premise this way:

> Everything has a purpose, or premise. Every second of our life has its own premise, whether or not we are conscious of it at the time. That premise may be as simple as breathing or as complex as a vital emotional decision, but it is always there. . . . Every good play must have a well-formulated premise.[2]

As noted by Egri, premises are derived from emotions—love, hate, fear, jealousy, desire, joy,

etc.—and usually involve a main character (protagonist), a conflict, and a conclusion. A good premise is a "thumbnail synopsis" of a story and can be expressed in a few words. For example, the premise of William Shakespeare's play *Othello* is "unchecked jealousy leads to death." Othello is the protagonist, his jealousy of wife Desdemona supplies the conflict, and death (of both) is the conclusion.

> **PROTAGONIST—**
> The main character in a story or narrative.

The premise of the Oscar-winning movie *The Silence of the Lambs* is "courage conquers evil." FBI agent Clarice Starling is the protagonist, her courage in confronting serial killer Buffalo Bill is the conflict, and his destruction is the conclusion. While the scene-by-scene action of the story revolves around Clarice's pursuit of the serial killer, the emotional center of piece, its conflict, is her fear. Clarice must conquer her fear and find her courage in order to defeat the evil of Buffalo Bill.

In the 2002 film *Spider-Man*, Spider-Man confronts the evil Green Goblin in a series of battles, but it is Spider-Man's love for Mary Jane that drives the story. Spider-Man must choose between loving Mary Jane as an ordinary young man, or as an emotionally distant superhero. Without the romance, the film would be the dramatic equivalent of a video game, visually stimulating but dramatically unsatisfying.

Premises can also be defined in terms of an overriding goal or need. In the *Lord of the Rings* trilogy, for example, the overriding goal is the destruction of the all-powerful Ring. Every event in the story happens directly or indirectly in the pursuit of that goal. Similarly, King Kong's goal in *King Kong* is the capture of actress Ann Darrow, the object of his desire.

According to screenwriter Pen Densham (*Robin Hood: Prince of Thieves*), "all stories are basically from exactly the same root . . . the most primary needs and experiences of the human animal."[3] Densham translates some of these basic needs into familiar story lines:

> . . . how to find a mate . . . Love stories.
>
> How to find food and survive . . . Disaster and treasure-hunting tales.
>
> How to avoid being hunted and killed . . . Murder mysteries and creature films—from *Jaws* to *Jurassic Park.*[4]

Most film premises relate to one main character and one conflict. Some movies, however, have multiple story lines connected by theme, time, or place. *American Beauty* and *Traffic*, for example, follow the lives of several different characters, each of whom has his or her own goal and conflict.

Other films feature multiple characters with a single goal. *Saving Private Ryan* focuses on a unit of soldiers, all of whom share the goal of survival. Not all of the men achieve the goal, but all must overcome their fears in order to attempt it.

One of the most popular film franchises of recent years, the Spider-Man movies are action packed. However, it is usually internal, emotional issues that drive the stories.

SENSORY STYLE

Actions speak louder than words. That adage applies to all creative writing, but is especially true of screenwriting. Like fiction, films can be set in any period and in any place, real or imaginary. They can focus on a single character, or dozens. Their characters can be completely silent or bursting with talk. Unlike in fiction, however, film stories are delivered directly through the viewers' eyes and ears, through actual sounds and images. According to screenwriter

Elijah Wood as Frodo in the penultimate scene of The Lord of the Rings: Return of the King *(2003).*

Ron Bass (*Rain Man, Snow Falling on Cedars*), "The difference between books and movies is that books are about what happens within people, and movies are about what happens *between* people."[5]

Another veteran screenwriter, Robert Benton (*Bonnie and Clyde, Places in the Heart*), explains the difference between film and fiction writing this way: "Films are very literal. For instance, if I say to you that on the way to work this morning I saw the most beautiful woman I ever laid eyes on, you will instantly pull up your idea of the most beautiful woman you can imagine. If I show you a photograph of that woman, you will know exactly what I mean—but you may or may not think she is as beautiful as I do."[6]

Screenwriting is often said to be visual, but a more accurate description would be "sensory." Screenwriters imagine their stories not only in pictures, but also in sounds—dialogue, music, and noises. As they write, they imagine the film playing out, almost as if it were being projected on a screen. They pretend to cast the actors, design the sets, place the camera, and determine the film's tempo. In short, they direct the story in their heads.

William Goldman (*Butch Cassidy and the Sundance Kid, Dreamcatcher*), who also writes novels, said about writing for the screen: "Movies are not about niceties of dialogue. Nice dialogue is better than dumb dialogue, but for the most part the camera's what you're writing for—and it's what the viewer is waiting for. The writer has to be a story-teller through the camera, and that's an odd skill."[7]

SHOWING VS. TELLING

As Goldman suggests, writing for the screen involves more than just stringing lines of dialogue together. With each scene, screenwriters must decide whether to tell their audience what is happening, or to show them. In a film, "telling" is done through dialogue and narration. Through spoken declarations, characters reveal what is happening to them, or what has happened to them in the past. "Showing," on the other hand, is achieved through the characters' actions and is conveyed primarily through images.

Most movies combine the art of telling with the art of showing. As a general rule, however, film is most effective when it shows rather than tells. For example, to suggest that character Jackie is upset at Marge for rustling her candy wrapper during a touching moment at the opera, a writer could have Jackie hiss, "Marge, be quiet!" Certainly Jackie's statement conveys her annoyance. A stronger, more memorable way to make the point, however, would be to have Jackie snatch the candy out of Marge's hand and toss it over the balcony. Jackie's actions leave a stronger imprint on the viewer's mind than her words.

This excerpt from the script of the 1946 film *It's a Wonderful Life* by Frances Goodrich, Albert Hackett,

The giant ape King Kong faces off against a deadly dinosaur in the 2005 film version of King Kong.

and Frank Capra offers another example of how writers show action:

> Living Room. George enters. The house is carpetless, empty—the rain and wind cause funny noises upstairs. A huge fire is burning in the fireplace. Near the fireplace a collection of packing boxes are heaped together in the shape of a small table and covered with a checkered oil cloth. It is set for two. A bucket with ice and a champagne bottle sit on a table as well as a bowl of caviar.

> A phonograph is playing on the box.
> It is playing "The Wedding March." . . .
> Mary is standing near the fireplace
> looking as pretty as any bride ever
> looked. She is smiling at George, who
> has been slowly taking in the whole
> set-up. Through a door he sees the
> end of a cheap bed, over the back of
> which is a pair of pajamas and a
> nightie.[8]

Without hearing a word of dialogue between George and Mary, the audience can easily figure out what is going on in this scene. The table set for two, the playing of "The Wedding March," and the pajamas and nightie on the bed are but a few details that reveal that George and Mary are newlyweds. Additionally, the image of the spare living room with packing boxes tells us that George and Mary have just moved in and own few possessions.

Through this series of images and sounds, the screenwriters have conveyed facts about the characters and have set a mood. Showing is not only a more engaging way to reveal information than telling, it also saves the filmmakers valuable screen time. In only a few seconds, the audience understands the setup of the scene.

POINT OF VIEW

Like chapters in a novel, every scene in a script is told from a particular point of view. Fiction writers convey point of view by the type of narration they choose to write—first-person, third-person, omniscient, etc. In fiction, point of view can change from section to section, but more often it remains the same throughout the story.

With movies, point of view is fluid, often changing within scenes, and is established both in the script and in production. Screenwriters, directors, and editors all contribute to a film's point of view. It can be conveyed directly through the camera—the audience sees the action as though looking through a certain character's eyes. It can also be suggested by which character dominates the action of a scene.

Writers convey point of view through the script's stage directions, or descriptive text. Occasionally a script will include specific camera angles, indicating from whose perspective a bit of action will be seen. In his script for the 1976 film *Taxi Driver*, Paul Schrader not only indicates a camera angle (POV SHOT or point-of-view shot) in the following scene, he also speaks directly to the reader:

> A lengthy POV SHOT from Travis' vantage point behind the wheel. We see the city as Travis sees it. The front windshield is a little dirty, the lighted meter just up at the low right screen. The intercom crackles with STATIC and MESSAGES.
>
> The light turns green; we take off with a start. A short first gear—quick shift— a long second gear. The cab eases to the right of the street, checking out prospective fares.

Our eyes scan the long lines of PEDESTRIANS. The regulars—bums, junkies, tourists, hookers, homosexuals, hippies—they mean nothing now. They only blend into the sidewalks and lighted storefronts.

Our eyes now concentrate on those that step away from the curb—is that man hailing a cab or scratching his head?[9]

At this point in the story, identification with the film's main character, Travis Bickle, is crucial. As much as possible, Schrader wants the reader to be inside Travis' head, to see the world as he sees it.

Robert De Niro as cab driver Travis Bickle in a scene from Taxi Driver (1976).

As the above scene demonstrates, screenwriters can suggest point of view by focusing on the activity of one character, or favoring one character over another in a given scene.

STRUCTURE

While fiction can be read and re-read over an indefinite period, a film or television show is designed to be viewed within a specific time frame. Movies usually run between 75 and 120 minutes, while television programs typically run from 30 to 120 minutes (commercial breaks included). DVDs notwithstanding, filmmakers today

> **THROUGH LINE—**
> The plot course of a film.

expect audiences to view their creations in one continuous sitting and create them accordingly.

To keep viewers in their seats, screenwriters structure their stories carefully from beginning to end. Structure is perhaps the most crucial element of any movie or television show. Dramas, comedies, miniseries, and shorts all have a distinct structure.

Classically structured movie stories are basically linear. They move forward chronologically, from point A to point B to point C, and so forth. These screenplays are like trains on a cross-country trip, with scheduled stops, a known destination, and an estimated arrival time. The journey's route, or through line, comes out of the story's premise. Every stop, or scene, gets the viewer closer to the desired destination. The through line comprises the core action of a film's story and is also known as its spine.

Nonclassically structured films like *Eternal Sunshine of the Spotless Mind* (2004) are put together like a tapestry or a jigsaw puzzle. They may jump around in time, from character to character, event to event. Even these nonlinear stories have a structure, however, as every scene is placed into the whole for the specific purpose of dramatizing the film's premise.

THE THREE-ACT STRUCTURE

A majority of screenplays employ a three-act structure. First used in ancient Greek drama, three-act dramatic structure became popular in American theater in the mid-twentieth century. Screenwriters, many of whom also worked in the theater, adopted the structure for the movies, and three acts has been the norm ever since.

Once a premise has been decided upon, screenwriters begin to sketch out the action of a story, its story line or plot. Although they may not break the plot into actual acts, as a playwright might, film writers usually imagine their stories in three parts.

In act one, main characters and conflicts are introduced. The conflict deepens in act two until it reaches a climax or breaking point. In act three, the conflict resolves and leads to a *denouement* or resolution. As a general rule, the second act is the longest, while act three is the shortest. In a two-hour, 120-page

DENOUEMENT—
The final outcome, or resolution, of a story.

24

script, for example, act one will run about forty pages; act two, fifty to sixty pages; act three, twenty to thirty pages.

The three-act structure of a typical romantic comedy could be stated simply as "boy meets girl, boy gets girl (act one); boy loses girl (act two); boy gets girl back (act three)." If the premise of the comedy is "love overcomes fear," then act one will not only set up the romantic relationship, it will also introduce the fear that will cause problems for the boy later on. Act one will also introduce the boy's rival, or the opposing force that will try to undo the relationship.

In act two, the romance will start to unravel, as the conflict—the boy's fear of commitment, say— asserts itself. The boy's fear, and how his rival uses that fear to his own advantage, will cause the romance to fall apart. By the end of act two, however, the boy will resolve to win the girl back and defeat his foe. In act three, the boy puts his plan into action and gets the girl back. In order to achieve his goal, however, he must overcome his fear.

During the film's second act, the conflict grows increasingly intense and complicated. This increased tension is called rising action. To keep tension going, writers devise obstacles to put in the main character's way, roadblocks that threaten to derail the train. In the "boy meets girl" story, act two obstacles might include not only the boy's rival, but meddling parents and work demands as well.

Whatever obstacles are chosen, the story should progress logically and organically. An organic plot development feels natural and inevitable, not forced by the writer. The viewer has to believe that, given what has come before, and what is known about the characters' lives, each movement in the plot makes sense and rings true.

Frank Pierson (*Dog Day Afternoon*, *Conspiracy*) described his approach to plot development this way: "Plot logic has to derive from the characters. The way I work is to think about a character who's gotten into a particular situation for himself, and then whatever comes out of that drives the next scene— and then I start the process over again to lead to the following scene. I always know what the end of the picture's going to be, but I never know exactly how I'm going to get there."[10]

THE TICKING CLOCK

Along with obstacles, screenwriters often create tension by imposing a deadline. The main character must complete an action by a certain date or time in order to achieve victory or avoid disaster. At points in the second act, the writer will remind the audience of the "ticking clock" looming over the characters, and thereby turn the heat up on them. The deadline in the "boy meets girl" story might be her impending engagement to the rival, or his scheduled departure for college.

Perhaps the most famous example of a "ticking clock" film is the 1952 release *High Noon*, written by Carl Foreman. In it, Sheriff Will Kane has ninety minutes to prepare for a confrontation with a deadly outlaw, who is arriving on the town's 12 P.M. train. Foreman heightened the tension of the deadline even further by having the action unravel more or less in real time—that is, by having the length of the movie be roughly equal to the length of the story.

THE TURNING POINT

The rising action of the script's second act reaches its peak, its climax, when the main character reaches a crucial moment of decision. In that decision, or turning point, the main character chooses between one of two actions. Once the decision is made, the character cannot go back, and everything that happens afterward, in act three, tumbles out of this decision. In the romantic comedy story, for example, the turning point might be the boy's decision to propose to the girl, a choice he had vigorously avoided in the past.

Once the boy proposes, the writer then has to reveal all the consequences of his decision. Does the girl accept? Does the wedding eventually take place? Does the rival try to sabotage the event? Does the boy get cold feet at the altar? Do they live happily ever after? Any or all of these questions might be dramatized in the film's third act.

The turning point in *It's a Wonderful Life* occurs when George Bailey, having seen what his home town would have become without him, decides not to commit suicide. All of the action of act two—the memories of George's past and his financial mishaps—builds to that moment on the bridge. Once George chooses to live, he must resolve the problems he had previously been trying to avoid. Because of what he has learned about himself in act two, however, he now has the courage to go on.

THE END

In revealing the fallout of the turning point, the third act brings together all the story threads of the previous two acts. A well-crafted script leaves no loose ends, and its conclusion feels inevitable. Movies often fall apart because what happens in the third act is inconsistent with what happened in acts one and two. Ideally, at the end of a movie the audience feels both a sense of completion and a curiosity about what will happen to the characters in the future.

SUBPLOTS

All full-length screenplays, especially traditionally structured scripts, contain at least one subplot. Subplots include the same elements as the main plot—character, conflict, and resolution. They have a beginning, middle, and end just like the main story, but they take up very little screen time. Although it used to be common to see subplots functioning only as comic relief, with little connection to the rest of the story, they now are expected to advance or enhance the main story. Subplots can either intersect with the main plot, affecting its outcome directly, or run parallel to it.

In *Million Dollar Baby* (2004), the relationship between gym manager Eddie Dupris and would-be boxer Danger Barch is a parallel subplot. How Eddie handles the mentally-challenged Danger and his boxing dreams does not directly impact the main story. It does, however, influence how the audience feels about the boxing world and those who aspire to be a part of it.

In the 2000 film *Gladiator*, the subplot romance between Roman General Maximus and Lucilla, the sister of his rival, Commodus, intersects with the main story of Maximus' revenge. Because Lucilla becomes involved in Maximus' attempts to overthrow her brother, the love story has a direct effect on the main plot. The romance itself, however, is not the key force in the drama.

SCENE STRUCTURE

Just as the screenplay as a whole has structure, so do individual scenes. Although a screenwriting rule-of-thumb states that scenes should not run more than two minutes (about two script pages), they still need to be shaped, with a beginning, middle, and end. In other words, each scene should work as a kind of minidrama within the whole.

Characters in each scene should have an objective, or need, and the tension created by these needs should rise throughout the scene. The moment at which the scene begins is called the point of attack. In general, screenwriters prefer to start a scene with the action or conversation in full swing, or as writer-director Michael Mann (*Miami Vice*, *The Insider*) puts it, "right into the middle of a rapidly flowing stream. They [the viewers] didn't tiptoe in from the bank; they're just—boom!—in it."[11]

Ideally, scenes end with buttons, little *denouements*, sealing off a scene with a punch. In television writing, buttons are used to lead the viewer into a commercial break. Depending of the film's genre, buttons can be comic—a punchline or gag—or suspenseful—the hero dangling from a cliff—anything that makes the viewer want to continue watching.

BACK STORY

Information about a character's past is called back story or exposition. As they plan their scripts, screenwriters create short biographies of their characters, describing everything from their birthplace to their favorite music. Screenwriters then choose which biographical details to include in the script based on the story's premise. Every screenplay contains back story because every character brings a certain amount of baggage to a drama. Even newborn babies have back stories—their parents.

Good exposition, like good plotting, flows naturally out of a situation, and screenwriters often

MOVIE GENRES

Just like fiction, films can be categorized by genre—a distinguishing form, style or setting. Drama, comedy, and comedy-drama comprise the three main genres. Some genres, like science fiction and horror, have loose rules that govern how they are executed. Many film stories combine genres. The 2004 film *The Village*, for example, is both a horror story and a mystery. *Eternal Sunshine of the Spotless Mind* combines romantic comedy with science fiction.

Over the decades, the popularity of certain genres has ebbed and flowed. Westerns used to be a movie-making staple but are rarely made today. They have been replaced by action-adventure films, which often have a science-fiction component. Teen movies were hot in the 1980s, but are much less prevalent today.

Below are some of the most common movie genres with examples of each:

1. Action-adventure (*Die Hard*)
2. Animation (*The Incredibles*)
3. Biographies (*Ray*)
4. Courtroom/Legal (*Runaway Jury*)
5. Documentary (*Super Size Me*)
6. Fantasy (*Lord of the Rings*)
7. Gangster (*The Godfather*)
8. Historical (*Troy*)
9. Horror (*The Ring*)
10. Mystery/Suspense (*Psycho*)
11. Police (*Serpico*)
12. Romantic comedy (*Notting Hill*)
13. Science fiction (*The Matrix*)
14. Social/Political (*Erin Brockovich*)
15. Sports (*Bad News Bears*)
16. Teen (*Ferris Bueller's Day Off*)
17. War (*Saving Private Ryan*)
18. Western (*The Unforgiven*)

devise scenes expressly for back story purposes. Facts about a person can be revealed through props, costumes, makeup, and behavior. In *Million Dollar Baby* the audience first suspects that boxing trainer Frankie Dunn has a troubled past when he finds a letter in his mail that has been marked "return to sender" and adds it to a bundle of similar letters. The letters imply that there is someone from Frankie's past who has rejected him.

Most back story is conveyed through dialogue. Getting-to-know-you scenes—in which two characters meet and exchange information about each other—are the easiest way to convey back story to the audience. Characters might meet on the first day of school, at a job interview, at a wedding or funeral, or at a bus stop. These situations provide a natural way for the audience to learn about the characters.

Back story can also be presented through flashbacks, scenes depicting moments from a character's past. Flashbacks, which can last a few seconds or comprise an entire scene, interrupt the ongoing action to comment on or enhance the story's conflict. As a general rule, writers use flashbacks when the action is too complicated to be effectively conveyed through dialogue.

Most exposition is revealed early in the script, but certain facts about a character may be withheld for dramatic effect. Secrets are the most powerful form of back story, and whole films can revolve around them.

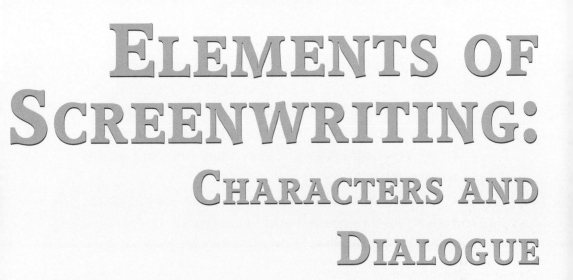

ELEMENTS OF SCREENWRITING:

CHARACTERS AND DIALOGUE

Whatever premise a screenwriter comes up with, the story must come from the characters' lives. The most admired screenplays are character driven, even those with complex plots. Alan Ball (*American Beauty*, *Six Feet Under*), a screenwriter known for quirky, character-driven stories, says: "The most interesting thing for me as a writer is and always has been character: people whose lives are complicated; people who are struggling to make the right choice in a morally ambiguous universe; people who are striving to live authentic lives in a world that is increasingly inauthentic."[1]

Characters define themselves through large

33

and small actions alike, through their words and their deeds. As in real life, movie characters have both a private and public side, the face they see in the mirror, and the one they present to the world. They may say one thing and do another. Their needs might be contradictory. Villains might be likable and heroes difficult.

As mentioned previously, to make their characters three-dimensional and believable, screenwriters often create profiles of them before starting on their story. These biographies include such facts as the character's physical traits—sex, age, race, general appearance; social and economic background— place of birth, occupation, education, and religion; and psychology—temperament, abilities, likes and dislikes, ambitions, moral standards, etc.

PROTAGONISTS AND ANTAGONISTS

Every good script begins and ends with the protagonist, or pivotal character. Simply put, the protagonist is the main character in a drama or literary work. Pivotal characters are often associated with goodness and greatness, but most modern-day protagonists are flawed and ordinary.

In classic film stories, what defines protagonists are not their inherent virtues, but their needs and desires. Directly or indirectly every action in a drama happens because of their needs and desires. According to Egri, the protagonist "is the one who creates conflict and makes the play move forward.

. . . A pivotal character must not merely desire something. He must want it so badly that he will destroy or be destroyed in the effort to attain his goal."[2]

What makes a good protagonist? Willfulness—the determination to make decisions and take actions—is the most important attribute of protagonists. Without it, protagonists appear weak, their actions inconsequential. Audiences quickly lose interest in a pivotal character who is unmotivated, indifferent or passive. Even comedies need an active protagonist.

Egri adds that "a good pivotal character *must have something very vital at stake*. . . . A man whose fear is greater than his desire, or a man who has no great, all-consuming passion, or one who has patience and does not oppose, cannot be a pivotal character."[3] Having great passion or drive does not mean that the protagonist never hesitates, however, or has no doubts or fears. Over the course of the story, a good protagonist struggles to overcome obstacles and achieve goals.

Generally speaking, a protagonist will be opposed by an antagonist. As Egri notes, the antagonist is the character against whom the protagonist "exerts all his strength, all his cunning, all the resources of his inventive power."[4] In most cases, the antagonist is easily identified as the "bad guy." His morals and motivations are clearly corrupt, his goals destructive.

In other stories, the antagonist's goals may be less sinister but will still pose the major obstacle for the protagonist. Antagonists do not have to be "bad" to be effective, but they do need to be as determined as the protagonist. To maintain interest, the audience must believe that the antagonist is capable of defeating the protagonist, even if the protagonist ultimately wins.

Nonhumans can be antagonists, but only if they have a certain level of intelligence. The creature in *Alien* and the shark in *Jaws* are both antagonists because they have control over their behavior—they choose to be bad. As a rule, though, animals and natural forces like tornadoes and earthquakes cannot function as antagonists.

SUPPORTING CHARACTERS

As their name implies, minor or supporting characters help the main characters achieve their goals, whether those goals are positive or negative. They can also add texture and depth to a scene. Often they are the key players in the story's subplots. Some may have significant screen time, appearing in many scenes throughout the film. Others may show up in only one scene.

To make their supporting characters easy to remember, screenwriters often give them obvious quirks or repeated bits of action. Physical mannerisms and habits, such as a nervous stutter or chain-smoking, are also used to differentiate minor characters.

Sigourney Weaver faces off against a terrifying antagonist in
Aliens (1986), the sequel to the very successful, earlier film
Alien (1979).

In Billy Wilder and I.A.L. Diamond's 1959 classic
Some Like It Hot, the ruthless gangster "Spats" is
known by his spotless spats shoes, while his
doomed rival, "Toothpick Charlie," is always seen
with a toothpick in his mouth.

Ted Elliott and Terry Rossio created a host of
notable supporting players for their 2003 hit *Pirates
of the Caribbean*—the pair of dimwitted English
soldiers, the goofy ghost pirates (one with a wooden
eye that pops out), the cowardly governor, even the

ghost captain's evil monkey. Though part of a very large cast, all these supporting characters stand out.

THE PROTAGONIST'S PROGRESS

Inherent in the premise of a story is character development. In order for the story's conflict to reach the turning point, protagonists must go through change. Their understanding of themselves and their place in the world must deepen in some way. They must learn and develop. Depending on the premise, they may develop in a positive way, or they may fall apart. This process of transformation is called the character arc. Character arcs are intertwined with the film's through line. As the plot progresses, so does the character.

In *Million Dollar Baby*, for example, Frankie Dunn begins as a self-doubting loner, separated from his family and friends. As he trains and grows closer to boxer Maggie Fitzgerald, Frankie becomes a more trusting, connected person. In his moment of decision, his newfound feelings are put to a life-or-death test. His final decision reflects the journey he has made as a character, and that journey, his arc, is represented by his actions.

At the start of the 1975 drama *One Flew Over the Cuckoo's Nest* by Bo Goldman and Lawrence Hauben, hero McMurphy gets himself locked up in a mental institution to avoid jail. McMurphy's motives are at first selfish; he cares only about his own needs. Gradually, however, he bonds with the other patients and joins with them against the villainous Nurse Ratched. In his moment of decision, McMurphy must choose between escaping the institution or confronting Ratched. Because he has learned to care about others, he decides to stay and fight, thereby sacrificing his longed-for freedom. Although his fate is terrible, he has become a hero in the eyes of the audience.

DIALOGUE

Unlike dialogue in fiction, movie dialogue is usually crisp and to-the-point. Good movie dialogue is a better version of everyday conversation. Real conversation tends to be disjointed and awkward, filled with cut-off sentences, repetitions, bad grammar, ramblings, interruptions, and pauses. Film dialogue retains the naturalism of everyday conversation, while removing most of the repetitions and awkwardness.

Through dialogue, screenwriters make characters authentic and three-dimensional. Well-written dialogue adds color and texture to the film's world. When creating characters, writers come up with a "voice," or a way of speaking, for each role. Character voices should reveal something about their background and experience. The speech of a young man should sound different from an old woman's, even if both characters come from the same place.

Johnny Depp as Captain Jack Sparrow in Pirates of the Caribbean *(2003). Both the lead and supporting characters in this film were fun and memorable.*

For the 1962 film *To Kill a Mockingbird*, screen-writer Horton Foote created a large palette of voices. Each character has his or her own speech patterns, quirks, and slang. The young Southern girl Scout always calls her father by his first name, Atticus, and utters grown-up expressions like "what in the Sam Hill." Atticus, a lawyer, is better educated than most of the people in his town, and his speech reflects his refinement. Strong regional accents are heard in some of the supporting characters, the "poor white folk." The African-American characters have yet another way of speaking. The blending of all these voices helps create the authentic world of the film.

CREATING TENSION THROUGH DIALOGUE

Every scene in a movie has its own rhythm or tempo, and dialogue is often its drumbeat. Tension within a scene can be heightened by quickening the tempo of a dialogue exchange. To speed up tempo, screen-writers will shorten character responses and increase the number of interruptions in a scene.

Many exchanges of dialogue work like an interrogation, with one character trying to extract information or concessions out of another. Questions create more tension than statements, because by posing them, a character can force an issue, demanding an answer from the other party. How the other party responds might surprise the questioning character and lead to more questions and conflict.

Heroes and Villians

In 2003, the American Film Institute, as part of its *100 Films . . .* series, compiled a list of the 100 greatest movie heroes and villains. Notice how many movies with "heroes" also have "villains."

Heroes
1. Atticus Finch (*To Kill a Mockingbird*)
2. Indiana Jones (*Raiders of the Lost Ark*)
3. James Bond (*Dr. No*)
4. Rick Blaine (*Casablanca*)
5. Will Kane (*High Noon*)
6. Clarice Starling (*The Silence of the Lambs*)
7. Rocky Balboa (*Rocky*)
8. Ellen Ripley (*Aliens*)
9. George Bailey (*It's a Wonderful Life*)
10. T. E. Lawrence (*Lawrence of Arabia*)
11. Jefferson Smith (*Mr. Smith Goes to Washington*)
12. Tom Joad (*Grapes of Wrath*)
13. Oskar Schindler (*Schindler's List*)
14. Han Solo (*Star Wars*)
15. Norma Rae Webster (*Norma Rae*)
16. Shane (*Shane*)
17. Harry Callahan (*Dirty Harry*)
18. Robin Hood (*The Adventures of Robin Hood*)
19. Virgil Tibbs (*In the Heat of the Night*)
20. Butch Cassidy and the Sundance Kid (*Butch Cassidy & the Sundance Kid*)
21. Mahatma Gandhi (*Gandhi*)
22. Spartacus (*Spartacus*)

23. Terry Malloy (*On the Waterfront*)
24. Thelma Dickerson and Louise Sawyer (*Thelma and Louise*)
25. Lou Gehrig (*The Pride of the Yankees*)

Villains

1. Dr. Hannibal Lecter (*The Silence of the Lambs*)
2. Norman Bates (*Psycho*)
3. Darth Vader (*The Empire Strikes Back*)
4. The Wicked Witch of the West (*The Wizard of Oz*)
5. Nurse Ratched (*One Flew Over the Cuckoo's Nest*)
6. Mr. Potter (*It's a Wonderful Life*)
7. Alex Forrest (*Fatal Attraction*)
8. Phyllis Dietrichson (*Double Indemnity*)
9. Regan MacNeil (*The Exorcist*)
10. The Queen (*Snow White and the Seven Dwarfs*)
11. Michael Corleone (*The Godfather, Part 2*)
12. Alex De Large (*Clockwork Orange*)
13. HAL 9000 (*2001: A Space Odyssey*)
14. The Alien (*Alien*)
15. Amon Goeth (*Schindler's List*)
16. Noah Cross (*Chinatown*)
17. Annie Wilkes (*Misery*)
18. The Shark (*Jaws*)
19. Captain Bligh (*Mutiny on the Bounty*)
20. Man (*Bambi*)
21. Mrs. John Iselin (*The Manchurian Candidate*)
22. Terminator (*The Terminator*)
23. Eve Harrington (*All About Eve*)
24. Gordon Gekko (*Wall Street*)
25. Jack Torrance (*The Shining*)

Danny De Vito, Jack Nicholson, Brad Dourif, and William Redfield (left to right) in a scene from One Flew Over the Cuckoo's Nest *(1976). Nicholson's character undergoes a stark transformation in becoming the film's "hero."*

The following excerpt from the beginning of Paul Schrader's *Taxi Driver* demonstrates the "interrogation" technique. In it, a personnel officer interviews Travis Bickle for a job driving a cab. In just a few seconds, the audience learns a lot about Travis:

TRAVIS
I'll work anywhere, any time. I know
I can't be choosy.

PERSONNEL OFFICER
(Thinks a moment)
How's your driving record?

TRAVIS
Clean. Real clean.
(Pause, thin smile.)
As clean as my conscience.

PERSONNEL OFFICER
Listen, son, you gonna get smart, you
can leave right now.

TRAVIS
(Apologetic)
Sorry, sir. I didn't mean that.

PERSONNEL OFFICER

Physical? Criminal?

TRAVIS
Also clean.

PERSONNEL OFFICER
Age?

TRAVIS
Twenty-six.

PERSONNEL OFFICER
Education?

TRAVIS
Some. Here and there.

PERSONNEL OFFICER
Military record?

TRAVIS
Honorable discharge. May, 1971.

PERSONNEL OFFICER
You moonlightin'?

TRAVIS
No, I want long shifts.[5]

In this exchange, Travis not only gives the personnel officer basic facts about himself, he also reveals a side of his personality that makes the officer uncomfortable. As the scene progresses, Schrader speeds up the tempo, and the tension, of the dialogue, with questions and answers coming rapidly. At the end of the scene, when the personnel officer puts his suspicions aside and hires Travis, the tempo of the dialogue slows back down.

PUTTING IT ALL TOGETHER:
ON THE WATERFRONT

Perhaps the most famous moment of the 1954 movie *On the Waterfront* is the "I could've been a contender" speech, delivered by a young Marlon Brando in the role of washed-up boxer Terry Malloy. Although Brando's poignant words have come to represent screen dialogue at its best, dialogue is but one component that makes Budd Schulberg's script a standout.

With its tight three-act structure and clear premise, *On the Waterfront* exemplifies Hollywood filmmaking at its best. The film, directed by the skillful veteran Elia Kazan, won eight Academy Awards, including Best Picture and Best Writing. It also stands as the number eight film on the top 100 movie list of the American Film Institute.

THE PREMISE

Note: The following analysis is based on the final shooting script of *On the Waterfront*, published in 1980. As is often the case, the screenplay differs somewhat from the actual film.

Though still in his twenties, Terry Malloy of Hoboken, New Jersey, is a has-been boxer, a waterfront "hanger-on." His older brother Charley (Rod Steiger) works for Johnny Friendly (Lee J. Cobb), a mobster who controls the Hoboken docks. Thanks to Charley, Terry receives preferential treatment from Johnny and Big Mac (James Westerfield), the local union hiring boss.

Johnny's favors to Terry come with a price, however. Johnny is being investigated by the government and has asked Terry to lure his friend, Joey Doyle, who is about to testify against Johnny, to a rooftop. There, Johnny's goons confront Joey and throw him off the roof to his death. Although he claims he did not know that the thugs intended to kill Joey, Terry is filled with guilt.

Terry's guilt intensifies when he encounters Joey's pretty sister Edie (Eva Marie Saint), a college student who is home on break. Unaware of Terry's involvement in Joey's murder, Edie encourages Terry to join Father Barry (Karl Malden), the parish priest, in fighting the mobsters. Despite his growing attraction for Edie, Terry is afraid to betray Johnny and does nothing to help.

Terry's emotional struggles come to a head after Johnny murders Charley and Edie learns the truth about Terry and her brother. Ultimately, Terry must choose between right and wrong, between doing nothing and risking his life.

On the Waterfront is the story of clashing opposites: purity vs. corruption; downfall vs. redemption; betrayal vs. loyalty; cowardice vs. courage. Most of all, however, it is a story about the power of love. In the end, Terry's love for Edie drives his decision to testify against Johnny and the mob. "Love conquers all" is, therefore, the film's premise.

CREATING A WORLD ON PAPER

Before he sat down to write the script for *On the Waterfront*, Schulberg researched his subject thoroughly. His initial inspiration for the story was a series of newspaper articles by Malcolm Johnson entitled "Crime on the Waterfront." Johnson's Pulitzer-Prize–winning articles, first published in 1948, chronicled real-life crime and corruption along New York's gritty waterfront.

In addition to reading Johnson's series, Schulberg went to the docks and got to know the people who lived and worked there. Several characters in the picture, including Father Barry and Kayo Nolan, were based on real people. Schulberg's hands-on research not only inspired his plot and character ideas, it also gave him an ear for the local speech and an eye for the local scenery.

Throughout his script, Schulberg uses settings—sights and sounds—and physical actions to advance and enhance the drama. With his very first scene, which opens on an exterior, night-time view of the New Jersey waterfront, Schulberg draws the reader into the story's world with precise, textured descriptions:

> A long, narrow wharf floating about twenty-five yards off shore, and on either side of the wharf are large ocean liners which are being unloaded by arc light. In the B.G. [background] is the glittering New York skyline. A great liner, blazing with light, is headed down river. A ferry chugs across to Manhattan. There is a counterpoint of ships' whistles, some shrill, others hauntingly muted.[1]

In this opening paragraph, Schulberg conveys to the reader a number of important details. First, he establishes the milieu in which the story takes place, not just the specific location—the New Jersey docks—but the atmosphere of the place as well. Even at night, the docks bustle with activity. One ship is being unloaded by arc light while other ships come and go. In addition, Schulberg contrasts the working-class wharf with the "glittering New York skyline," which he places in the background.

Schulberg then introduces his protagonist, Terry Malloy:

> Coming along the gangplank toward the shore is an isolated figure. He is TERRY MALLOY, a wiry,

jaunty, waterfront hanger-on in his late twenties. He wears a turtleneck sweater, a windbreaker and a cap. He whistles a familiar Irish song.[2]

Right from the start, Schulberg shows Terry as a loner, "an isolated figure." Even before Terry's social isolation becomes an issue in the drama, Schulberg suggests it visually. Through his description of Terry's clothes and Irish song whistling, Schulberg also reveals that his protagonist is working class. He is a product of this blue-collar world, even as he is isolated from it.

A few pages later, after Joey's murder, Schulberg has Terry retreating to the Friendly Bar, a local hangout:

It is a rough waterfront bar full of half-gassed longshoremen and pistol boys. They are all watching a fight on TV above the bar, and there is much hoarse laughter and ad lib jokes at the fight. The only one not watching is Terry, who sits at a table by himself staring at a half-finished glass of beer.[3]

Schulberg establishes the bar as a place where dock workers, union bosses, and mobsters converge. Although a social gathering place, the bar is anything but "friendly." Again, Schulberg segregates Terry, literally and figuratively. Terry's mounting guilt and confusion is demonstrated through his actions—he sits alone, staring downward, not participating in the group activity. Schulberg does not need to tell the audience how

Terry is feeling. The viewer can sense his inner turmoil through his body language.

Schulberg then contrasts the Friendly Bar with the neighborhood Catholic church, where Father Barry has called an impromptu meeting. There, as Terry, who has been sent by Johnny to spy on the proceedings, looks on, Father Barry tries to persuade the dockworkers to identify Joey's killers. The men are too terrified to speak up, however, and Father Barry's conservative superior, Father Vincent, warns against using the church to fight the mob.

Compared to the bar, the church setting, with its stained-glass windows and figures of saints, is warm and welcoming. During the meeting, however, a rock is hurled through one of the windows, and thugs later attack the workers as they are leaving the church. Despite the contrast with Friendly's, Schulberg makes clear that the church is not a true sanctuary for the workers.

Another important location in the movie is the rooftop of Terry's apartment building, where Terry raises pigeons:

> Autumn on the roof. It is not particularly romantic—there are clotheslines, wooden boxes, etc. But to the people of this neighborhood it is a luxurious terrace. Terry's birds are aloft, flying in a great circle, nicely silhouetted against the sun-drenched evening sky. . . .Terry has a long pole with which he keeps the birds flying.[4]

In one sense, the rooftop and the pigeons suggest the openness and freedom which Terry and the other dockside residents desire. Like the church setting, however, the rooftop also represents violence and entrapment. It is, after all, where Joey is cornered and killed. Terry's pigeons can fly, but they are also controlled by a pole and are kept in wire coops. Just as Terry is trapped and controlled by

Terry (Marlon Brando) shows Edie (Eva Marie Saint) the pigeon coop he keeps on the roof of his apartment building in a scene from On the Waterfront *(1954).*

the mob, the pigeons are trapped and controlled by Terry.

STRUCTURE AND POINT OF VIEW

The Opening Round

Although there are no formal act breaks in *On the Waterfront*, the film is roughly organized into a three-act structure. Schulberg uses this structure to bring his premise to life.

Like all good screenwriters, Schulberg wastes no time setting up the main conflict of the film. By having Joey killed within the first minute of screen time, Schulberg makes clear what type of story he is telling and immediately hooks the viewer into the drama. The audience does not need to know exactly who Terry and Joey are, or why Joey is being pursued by the thugs in order to appreciate the danger and treachery of their world. Right from the start, the viewer understands that the stakes are life and death.

Through his stage directions, Schulberg also establishes Terry as the film's point-of-view character. The audience experiences the action primarily through Terry's eyes and ears, as shown in the following passage from the film's opening sequence, during which Joey goes up to the tenement roof to meet Terry, who is on the street, holding one of Joey's pigeons:

> Tensely, as if going through something he wishes
> he could avoid, Terry looks in the direction of the

tenement stoop and nods. Now for the first time we see two men standing there under the doorway so that Joey was unable to see them from his window. When Terry nods they enter the tenement hallway; he takes a few steps forward so as to be out of sight from Joey's window. Then Terry raises the pigeon into the air and, inexplicitly, releases it. As it wings out of sight he turns and starts in the direction from which he came, walking crabwise as if trying to see the effect of what he has just done.[5]

Schulberg creates point of view by staying focused on Terry's actions and reactions. The scene easily could have been written from Joey's point of view, as he first interacts with Terry and then with the thugs. If it had been told from Joey's point of view, the audience would have been blind to the thugs lurking in the doorway and would have been startled, along with Joey, by their sudden appearance.

Instead, the audience follows Terry, pulling away from the building as soon as he alerts the thugs. Although Schulberg later dramatizes some of the assault, he cuts back to Terry before the actual murder to show his reaction to Joey's death scream. In this way, Schulberg forces the viewer to identify with Terry, even as he is committing an act of betrayal.

In addition to Terry, Schulberg introduces the other main characters within the first ten pages of the script—Edie, Father Barry, Johnny Friendly, and

Terry's brother Charley. Also in the first few pages, Schulberg establishes the dynamic between Johnny and Terry. Johnny is shown as the corrupt but fearless leader, while Terry is his reluctant but obedient helper.

The first act exposes Johnny's illegal operations and the government crime commission that is investigating them. In one dramatic scene, Schulberg shows how Big Mac, the hiring boss, forces the dockworkers to fight with one another for that day's work assignments. The Crime Commission hearings, which the audience learns are coming up, creates a deadline in the story. The first act also sets up the love affair between Edie and Terry. Schulberg makes these getting-to-know-you scenes tense, as Terry is struggling to keep his involvement with Johnny a secret from Edie.

The film's first act ends after Terry asks Edie if they can see each other again, and Edie announces to her father that she is staying in Hoboken until she uncovers the identity of Joey's murderer. For both characters, the wheels of change have been set into motion.

Act Two

Act two begins on Terry and Edie's first formal date. Schulberg uses this sequence to reveal key psychological information and the back story for his main characters. For example, as the couple questions each other over beers, Terry admits to Edie that during his boxing days, he "took dives" for Johnny. This confession helps the audience understand Terry's long-standing relationship with Johnny and explains his lack of self-esteem.

During the same scene, Schulberg has Terry state his "do-it-to-him-before-he-does-it-to-you" philosophy, which Edie denounces. Although Terry's attitude echoes the general sentiment of the docks, Edie senses that Terry is capable of greater things. Her innocent faith in him moves Terry, even as he declines to stick his neck out for her.

Throughout the second act, Schulberg deepens the connection between Terry and Edie, while complicating Terry's position with Johnny and the Crime Commission. With each step Terry takes toward Edie, he is yanked back by Johnny, and spun around by the government agents.

At the end of the date sequence, for instance, as Terry is walking Edie home, one of Johnny's flunkies approaches him with orders to report immediately to Johnny. In defiance, Terry sends the underling away but is clearly unnerved by the situation:

                    TERRY
                 (impulsively)
        Edie, listen, stay out of this mess.
        Quit tryin' to ask things about Joey.
        It ain't safe for you.

                    EDIE
        Why worry about me? You're the one
        who says only look out for yourself.

57

                    TERRY
        (pent up with his guilt and his
          frustrated feeling for her)
    Okay, get in hot water. But don't come
    hollerin' to me when you get burned.

                    EDIE
    Why should I come hollering to you at
    all?

                    TERRY
    Because . . . because. . . .
        (apologetically, as if this were a
              sign of weakness)
    Listen, Edie, don't get sore now—but
    I think we're getting in love with
    each other.

                    EDIE
        (really fighting against it)
    I can't let myself fall in love with you.

                    TERRY
              (fervently)
    That goes double for me.

As they stare at each other in entangled hostility
and love, a man turns from the food counter behind
them, just finishing a hot dog and steps into Terry's
path. It is Mr. Glover, the Commission investigator.[6]

Glover then serves Terry with a subpoena,
compelling him to appear at the Crime Commission
hearings.

As the hearing nears, Johnny arranges for longshoreman Kayo Nolan, who is about to testify against him, to be "accidentally" killed while on the job. Nolan's death drives Terry to confess all to Father Barry. At Father Barry's urging, Terry also confesses to Edie, who runs from him in tears. Glover then applies more pressure on Terry to "name names." Scene by scene in act two, Schulberg builds tension, increases the stakes, and turns the screws on Terry.

At this point, the arc of the script is reaching its zenith. The goal of act two is to get Terry to his moment of decision, his turning point. He knows that if he testifies against Johnny, he will not only be labeled a traitor by some, but his life will be in danger as well.

Aware that Terry has been subpoenaed, Johnny orders Charley to straighten his brother out, one way or the other. Although Charley recoils at the idea of setting Terry up, he knows that his own life is at stake if he refuses. Charley picks Terry up in a cab and, while riding with him, tries to convince him to play dumb at the Crime Commission hearing by offering him a plum job on the docks. When Terry hesitates, Charley pulls a gun, and Terry realizes that his brother is about to do to him what he did to Joey.

Terry finally understands that while he loves Charley, Charley's loyalty has always lain with Johnny. While recalling his boxing days, Terry finally starts to connect the past with the present and condemns both himself and Charley:

> TERRY
> You don't understand! I could've been a contender. I could've had class and been somebody. Real class. Instead of a bum, let's face it, which is what I am. It was you, Charley. . . . It was you, Charley. . . .[7]

Moved by his brother's words, Charley allows him to escape, advising him to "jump out, quick, and keep going."

Desperate, Terry breaks down Edie's door and declares his love for her. Though still angry and confused, Edie gives in to her feelings and kisses Terry. Their embrace is interrupted when Terry is summoned to the street by Johnny's men.

There, Terry discovers Charley's body. Enraged at his brother's murder, Terry breaks into a pawnshop and steals a gun. As Edie pleads with him to stop, Terry storms off to the Friendly Bar to confront Johnny. Before he can, Father Barry finds him and challenges him to drop the gun and do the right thing:

> FATHER BARRY
> . . . You want to be brave? Firing lead into another man's flesh isn't brave.
> . . . You want to hurt Johnny Friendly?. . . Don't fight him like a

***Eva Marie Saint as Edie in a scene from* On the Waterfront.**

hoodlum down here in the jungle. . . .
Fight him tomorrow in the
courtroom—with the truth as you
know it—Truth is the gun . . .[8]

The second act ends as Terry heeds Father Barry
and makes up his mind to testify. Unable to turn
back, Terry has reached his moment of decision.

The Last Act

The next day, Terry appears at the hearing and implicates Johnny in Joey's murder. Afterward, Johnny threatens Terry, and the dockworkers snub him as a traitor. Terry also discovers that his teenage friend Jimmy has killed all of his pigeons in anger over his testimony. Concerned for Terry's safety, Edie suggests that Terry flee, but Terry marches to the docks to tell Johnny he will not be intimidated.

Aware that the authorities are watching him, Johnny hides his guns and challenges Terry to a fight. As Terry is about to finish Johnny off with his fists, Johnny's thugs jump in and pummel Terry senseless. Edie and Father Barry rush to Terry's side, and when Johnny yells at Edie's father to get to work, Pop screws up his courage and pushes Johnny into the water. Inspired by Terry's and Pop's bravery, the other longshoremen then refuse to work until Terry does.

Sensing the symbolic importance of the situation, Father Barry urges the half-conscious Terry to get to his feet. As Terry staggers down the pier, the others fall in behind him, and Terry's transformation from follower to leader is complete:

> As Father Barry and Edie look on, Stevedore blows his whistle for work to begin. Longshoremen by the hundreds march into the pier behind Terry like a conquering army. In the B.G. a frenzied Johnny Friendly is still screaming, "I'll be back! I'll be back!"

The threat, real as it is, is lost in the forward progress of Terry and the ragtail army of dockworkers he now leads.[9]

Schulberg could have ended the picture right after Terry's damning testimony. Instead, he returns to the docks, where the last test of Terry's courage takes place. Terry's knock-down fight with Johnny satisfies the audience's desire for an exciting confrontation between good and evil. It allows Terry a face-to-face showdown with his nemesis, something that a mere arrest would not supply. Just as important, the last scene shows the entire wharf community reforming and rising up with Terry.

CHARACTERS AND DIALOGUE

Protagonist and Antagonist

Who is the protagonist of *On the Waterfront*? Although Edie is an important character, she is not the story's protagonist. Neither is Father Barry. While both are "good" and both initiate action, neither one goes through a significant change or development. Terry, however, does.

Similarly, although Schulberg includes a mysterious character named "Mr. Upstairs," a powerful, rich man who gives orders to Johnny Friendly, he is not the film's antagonist. Johnny Friendly is.

Terry is a strong protagonist because he is both flawed and heroic. If Terry demonstrated the same courage that Joey does—if he defied Johnny right from the start—he would be an admirable human being but a boring protagonist. At the same time, if Terry lacked the potential for sacrifice and courage, he could not grow as a character. His emotional struggles power the film's plot. Without them, the story would have nowhere to go.

Johnny works as a character for the same reason that Terry does, but in reverse. Schulberg reveals early on that Johnny, like Terry, had a rough, loveless childhood. Through effort and determination, Johnny fought his way out of poverty to the top of the mob hierarchy. Where Terry is confused and waffling, Johnny is confident and forceful. Unlike Terry, however, Johnny has no conscience or compassion, no potential for good. Consequently, as Terry grows stronger, Johnny weakens.

Supporting Characters

Along with his powerful main characters, Schulberg includes many effective supporting roles in his story. Edie, Father Barry, Charley, Pop (Edie's father), Jimmy, and Nolan are all key secondary characters. They help move the story and add texture to the wharf arena.

The most significant supporting character is Edie. Without her, there would be no story. As the object of Terry's love, Edie supplies the motivation for his behavior. She also becomes a positive role model for Terry. Although Terry feels immediate guilt about Joey's death, it is Edie's plea for help that starts the real struggle with his conscience. He wants to be "deaf and dumb" like the other longshoremen, but he also wants Edie's approval and attention. In the end, his desire to please and impress Edie causes Terry to defy Johnny, and that in turn, leads to Charley's murder and Terry's decision to testify.

While Edie inspires Terry throughout the story, Father Barry and Charley are his counterweights. They offer opposing counsel to Terry, the outward manifestations of his internal struggle. The priest appeals to Terry's better instinct, while Charley, the older brother who encouraged Terry to take boxing "dives," to lose fights on purpose, appeals to his bad side.

Father Barry represents moral society, the ideals by which good citizens live. As the dilemma in the story revolves around a social crisis—the mob's control over the docks—Father Barry's views are particularly important. Father Barry's willingness to defy his superior and stand up to the mob supplies the foundation for Terry's resistance. He urges not just Terry to be a better person, but the entire community as well.

Another memorable supporting character is Mutt Murphy, the one-armed dockside bum. Although he appears briefly in only a few scenes, Mutt is an important foil to Terry. He is Terry's emotional mirror, the personal voice of his conscience. While Mutt may look like a bum, Terry is a bum in spirit. Mutt says out loud what Terry feels inside.

In Schulberg's screenplay, Mutt first appears early on, as Terry is about to lure Joey onto the rooftop. Later, Terry and Edie encounter Mutt on the street when he asks them for a dime. Recognizing Edie as Joey's sister, Mutt praises Joey as a "saint"

Marlon Brando stands between presenter Bette Davis and fellow Oscar winner Grace Kelly at the 1955 Academy Awards. Brando won "Best Actor" for his portrayal of Terry in **On the Waterfront.**

and hints that Terry was "there" the night Joey was murdered. To keep Mutt quiet, Terry shoves a fifty-cent piece into his hand.

> MUTT
> I can't believe it—a small fortune.
> (He kisses the coin, then pulls from
> his shirt a small tobacco pouchful of
> coins in which he deposits this one.)
> (then turns on Terry again)
> You can't buy me—you're still a bum!
> (raises his cap to Edie with
> unexpected formality)
> 'Bye, Edie. Lord have mercy on Joey.
> (crosses himself quickly
> and he goes off)[10]

In this brief exchange, Schulberg conveys a lot of information about Mutt and his relationship with Terry. He makes Mutt come alive as a minor character. Mutt is both tough and gentle, crude and refined, deluded and sharp. Terry does everything he can to silence Mutt, but like his conscience, can never completely get rid of him.

DIALOGUE

While researching the people he was writing about, Schulberg noted quirks and tendencies in their speech. Most of his characters, like Johnny, use rough, colloquial language.

JOHNNY
Listen kid, I'm a soft touch too. Ask
any rummy on the dock if I'm not
good for a fin any time they put the
arm on me.
       (then more harshly)
But my old lady raised us ten kids on
a stinkin' watchman's pension. When
I was sixteen I had to beg for work in
the hold. I didn't work up out of
there for nuthin.'[11]

Terry's speech is peppered with youthful slang and boxing references. Although he and Edie grew up in the same working-class neighborhood, Edie's father sheltered her and sent her off to college. As a result, Edie is not only more educated than Terry, she is also more refined and innocent.

COLLOQUIAL—
Characteristic of
informal speech or
conversation.

Schulberg demonstrates the differences between the two in the following exchange, which takes place at the Friendly Bar. There, bartender Al serves beer to Terry and the wide-eyed Edie:

EDIE
Were you really a prizefighter?

TERRY
(nods)
I went pretty good for a while, didn't I,
Al? But—I didn't stay in shape—and—

68

(a little ashamed)
—I had to take a few dives.

EDIE
A dive? You mean, into the water?

TERRY
(laughs harshly)
Naw, in the ring, a dive is—

He stops, shakes his head and with his
finger draws an invisible square in the air.

EDIE
(mystified)
Now what are you doing?

TERRY
Describing you. A square from out
there. I mean you're nowhere.
(draws it again)
Miss Four Corners.[12]

In just a few lines of dialogue, Schulberg distinguishes his characters' backgrounds through their choice of words and their gestures.

Terry's dialogue includes slang and bad grammar, while Edie's language is straightforward and correct. Father Barry's speech also reflects his background. As a priest, he is educated but retains much of the roughness of his youth. He uses this roughness to connect with his parishioners.

THE ART OF COLLABORATION

Without a doubt, screenwriters are the loneliest members of the filmmaking process. Unlike producers, directors, actors, editors, art directors, and other crew members, screenwriters do most of their creating alone. Once a script has caught the attention of a production company, however, the writer usually (but not always) begins a series of rewrites involving others.

Because producers supply the money to make a picture, writers must first satisfy them. In this phase, referred to as "in development," writers and producers collaborate on the overall effectiveness of the story. Character arcs and turning points might be altered, openings and endings reworked, dialogue sharpened.

Quite often, after buying the screenplay, producers bring in other writers to do rewrites. Sometimes the original writer is replaced, or shunted to the side once production begins. If the writer is lucky, however, he or she will team up with a director and collaborate on bringing the script to the big screen.

Budd Schulberg was one of the lucky writers. Over a two-year period, he and director Elia "Gadg" Kazan worked closely on the script, from first to final draft. Theirs was a respectful, lively collaboration. "Out of day-and-night talkfests at my farm and his house on 72nd Street," Schulberg wrote, "we thrashed out the characters, the story line, the theme."[13]

During production, Schulberg recalled, Kazan kept his promise not to change the script. "Oh sure, lines overlapped, good, fresh words were thrown in spontaneously, but scene by scene Gadg stuck to the script, inventing and improving with staging that surprised and delighted me."[14] Schulberg obviously was not the only one delighted. *On the Waterfront* went on to become one of America's favorite movies.

During the church meeting with the dockworkers, for example, Father Barry mixes biblical references with slang.

> FATHER BARRY
> (rapidly, with a cigarette
> in his mouth)
> I thought there'd be more of you here,
> but—the Romans found what a
> handful could do, if it's the right
> handful. And the same
> goes for you and the mob that's got
> their foot on your neck. I'm just a
> potato-eater but isn't it simple as one-
> two-three? One—The working
> conditions are bad. Two—They're bad
> because the mob does the hiring.
> Three—The only way to break the
> mob is to stop letting them get away
> with murder.[15]

In contrast to the others, the speech of Father Barry's superior, Father Vincent, and the two Crime Commission investigators, Glover and Gillette, is smooth and refined. They are outsiders, as their words clearly show.

PUTTING IT ALL TOGETHER:
THE BREAKFAST CLUB

John Hughes's 1985 comedy-drama *The Breakfast Club* has been called the quintessential 1980s film. For audiences of the time, *The Breakfast Club* dramatized everything that was good and bad about the "me" decade—self-absorption vs. self-examination, conformity vs. rebellion, materialism vs. idealism. Along with Hughes's 1986 hit, *Ferris Bueller's Day Off*, the film represents a high point in a genre that became hugely popular in the 1980s: the teen movie.

The success of the film pushed its stars—Molly Ringwald, Emilio Estevez, Judd Nelson, Ally Sheedy, and Anthony Michael Hall—into the Hollywood limelight. Because they were close in age and were often cast in the same films, critics labeled them the "Brat Pack."

Today, the film still resonates with young audiences. Hughes translated the inner turmoil of the teenage mind into universal characters that transcend period.

Note: The following analysis is based on a transcription of the film's dialogue.

PREMISE

As the opening narration reveals, *The Breakfast Club* is the story of five high school students, "a brain, an athlete, a basket case, a princess, and a criminal."[1] Each character—Brian, the brain; Andrew, the athlete; Allison, the basket case; Claire, the princess; and Bender, the criminal—has been ordered by teacher Richard Vernon to spend an entire Saturday in detention. Vernon confines the students to the school library and assigns them to write a one thousand word essay on "who you think you are."

The five students, each of whom is in detention for a different reason, spend the next nine hours together. As the day progresses, the teens open up and learn some surprising truths about themselves. Although each teen is unique, they are united by their fears and confusion. Through their interactions, they come to understand their own problems and to open their eyes to the plight of the others.

The teens' stories are connected by a common theme: acceptance. All of the teens yearn for understanding and acceptance, both from the adults in their lives and from one another. Their need for acceptance fuels their behavior and ultimately leads to change. In order to find acceptance, they must overcome their fears—fear of rejection and of the unknown. The premise of *The Breakfast Club* is "acceptance overcomes fear."

STRUCTURE AND POINT OF VIEW

Stylistically *The Breakfast Club* is very different from *On the Waterfront*. Where the earlier movie exemplifies classic cinematic storytelling, *The Breakfast Club* is less traditional in its approach. Instead of a single protagonist, it has five, and instead of a driving three-act structure, the plot is loosely constructed around the events of a single day. The structure nonetheless works to support the story's premise.

Morning

Hughes opens the film with voice-over narration (V.O.), spoken by character Brian Johnson (Anthony Michael Hall), over shots of a suburban high school:

> BRIAN
> (V.O.)
> Saturday . . . March 24, 1984.
> Shermer High School, Shermer,
> Illinois. 60062. Dear Mr. Vernon . . .
> we accept the fact that we had to
> sacrifice a whole Saturday in
> detention for whatever it was that we

did wrong, what we did was wrong.
But we think you're crazy to make us
write this essay telling you who we
think we are, what do you care? You
see us as you want to see us . . . in
the simplest terms and the most
convenient definitions. You see us as
a brain, an athlete, a basket case, a
princess, and a criminal. Correct?
That's the way we saw each other at
seven o'clock this morning. We were
brainwashed.[2]

The narration not only tells the audience who and what the characters are, and where and when the story takes place, it also suggests how the story will unfold. Although the school shots appear to be from the present, the narration comes from the end of the story. Right off, Hughes reveals that the story will conclude at the end of the day and that the conflict will involve the students and teacher Richard Vernon (Paul Gleason).

Over the next two minutes, Hughes introduces all of his main characters. Each student is seen briefly as he or she arrives at school. The first to pull up is pretty, snobbish Claire (Molly Ringwald), who complains to her indulgent father about getting detention for skipping school to go shopping.

The nerdish Brian arrives next with his mother and little sister. After Mrs. Johnson dismisses Brian with a stern order to study during detention, the jock, Andrew, (Emilio Estevez), drives up with his father.

Andrew's dad scolds him for getting caught while "screwing around" and warns him not to become a "discipline case." John Bender (Judd Nelson) then strolls up. Bender, in sunglasses, walks in front of a beat-up car, causing the driver to slam on the brakes. Scruffy Allison (Ally Sheedy), dressed all in black, gets out of the car and scurries into school.

Once the teens are seated in the school library, Vernon walks in and announces the rules for the detention: no talking, no getting up, and no sleeping. Immediately, Vernon lock horns with the back-talking Bender and issues him a special warning. After Vernon retreats to his office across the hall, the teens begin to size up one another. Walking and talking, Bender wastes no time violating Vernon's rules and encourages the others to follow suit.

The film's early scenes play out like a verbal dance, with each character circling and prodding the others. The teens talk about school, sex, and drugs. While Bender insults everyone in turn, "straight-A" student Brian tries to calm the waters with his naïve observations. Claire deflects Bender's sexually charged remarks, and Andrew tries to maintain his macho image. Allison says nothing, but makes her presence known through theatrical gestures. At the same time, the group tries to outwit Vernon.

By midmorning, the teens' natural antagonism towards one another boils over. Andrew and Bender come to blows over Claire, and Bender threatens Andrew with a switchblade. After Andrew tosses him

Mr. Vernon (played by Paul Gleason) lays down the law to his students in one of the early scenes of The Breakfast Club *(1985).*

to the ground with a wrestling move, Bender retreats, and the tension is relieved by the appearance of the janitor, Carl (John Kapelos).

Lunchtime

At lunchtime, Vernon allows Allison and Andrew to leave the library to get drinks for the group. Alone with Andrew, Allison finally speaks, declaring that her favorite drink is vodka. Each asks the other why they are in detention but neither one is willing to answer. Back in the library, Bender teases Brian about his sex life and gets him to admit in front of Claire that he is a virgin. To Bender's surprise, Claire, whose parents are about to divorce, is impressed.

During the lunch-eating scene, Hughes raises the heat on the teens even higher. After Bender teases Brian about his all-American family, Andrew dares Bender to talk about his family. Bender lets loose with a snarling imitation of his abusive parents and shows the group a scar left by his father's lit cigar. Bender's confession stuns the others into silence.

The silence soon ends, however, after Vernon leaves his office and Bender sneaks the group to his locker to retrieve his baggie of marijuana. When Vernon is spotted, Bender gives Brian his dope, then becomes a decoy. Vernon chases Bender into the gymnasium, while the others run back to the library undetected.

Fed up with Bender's defiance, Vernon drags him to a utility closet. There Vernon challenges Bender, who is in detention for pulling the school's fire alarm, to fight him. When Bender declines, Vernon calls him a "gutless turd." Vernon locks Bender in, but Bender escapes by climbing into the overhead heating duct.

Somewhere over the library, the heating duct gives way and Bender crashes through the ceiling. Hearing the noise, Vernon rushes in. The teens

Molly Ringwald (as Claire), Judd Nelson (as Bender), and Anthony Michael Hall (as Brian) in a scene from The Breakfast Club.

conspire to hide Bender, and Vernon leaves, unaware that Bender is no longer in the closet.

Afternoon

Bender's near miss brings the teens a little closer together. They begin slowly to relax and reveal secrets about themselves, peeling off the remains of their emotional armor. Although the dialogue maintains its comic edge, Hughes darkens the overall tone of the film through this section.

First Allison confesses to Andrew and Brian that she keeps her purse filled with supplies in case she needs to run away from her "unsatisfying" home life. When Andrew, concerned, presses her to explain, Allison cries and admits that her parents "ignore" her. While not revealing anything himself, Andrew cries along with her.

In front of the others, Allison then brags that she is a nymphomaniac. Allison's claim disturbs Claire, who is finally forced to reveal she is a virgin like Brian. After Claire confesses, Allison announces she is actually a virgin, too—and a compulsive liar.

Andrew then reveals that he is in detention because he bullied and humiliated another student. Andrew, who up until this point has avoided questions about his family, then lets loose with a long, tearful tirade against his father:

ANDREW
And the bizarre thing is, is that I did
it for my old man . . . I tortured this

81

poor kid, because I wanted him to
think that I was cool. He's always
going off about, you know, when he
was in school . . . all the wild things
he used to do. And I got the feeling
that he was disappointed that I never
cut loose on anyone, right. . . . he's
like this mindless machine that I
can't even relate to anymore. . .
"Andrew, you've got to be number
one! I won't tolerate any losers in
this family . . ."[3]

Inspired by Andrew's honesty, Brian declares that he is miserable because he is about to fail shop class and lose his perfect grade-point average. "When I look in at myself," he says, "and I see me . . . I don't like what I see, I really don't."[4]

When Brian later wonders whether any of them will acknowledge the others come Monday, Claire again infuriates Bender by saying no. Claire insists she is merely being honest and complains that her other friendships are painfully shallow.

Brian then discloses that he is serving detention for bringing a gun to school. Brian explains that he could not deal with his failing grade and was contemplating using the gun to kill himself. After Brian reveals that it was a flare gun and that it went off in his locker, the others burst into laughter. Allison then confesses that she came to detention because she had nothing better to do.

Dismissal

With all the teens' secrets out, Hughes relaxes the pace of the film, allowing the relationships to play out in the *denouement.* After Brian agrees to write the essay for the group, Bender crawls back through the heating duct to the utility closet. Claire does a quick beauty makeover on Allison, who stuns Andrew with her new look. Claire then finds Bender in the closet and kisses him. The day is done, and the teens go their separate ways, but not before Claire gives Bender one of her diamond earrings, and Allison steals a patch from Andrew's letter jacket.

Hughes concludes by returning to the essay and Brian's voice-over from the opening of the film. Brian declares that while Vernon sees them in the "simplest terms," they have discovered that each one of them is, in their own way, "a brain, and an athlete, and a basket case, [and] a princess and a criminal."[5]

POINT OF VIEW

Unlike *On the Waterfront*, which presents a majority of scenes from Terry's point of view, in *The Breakfast Club* point of view does not favor one character over another. In literature, this type of point of view is called omniscient. The story's narrator describes and comments on the action from a distance, with no attempt to get inside a character's head. Screenwriters create an omniscient point of view by using few or no point-of-view shots and by making descriptive text neutral.

Sitting together on the library floor and talking, the characters of The Breakfast Club *will change and grow based on their interaction.*

CHARACTER AND DIALOGUE

Ensemble Casting

As the opening of the film suggests, *The Breakfast Club* features an ensemble cast, that is, a cast not dominated by a single character. Allison, Andrew, Bender, Brian, and Claire represent the spectrum of teen personalities, the kinds of teens found in most high schools: the misfit loner; the jock; the delinquent; the nerd; the prom queen. The teacher,

Richard Vernon, is also a familiar type—the petty dictator. Hughes takes these familiar characters and makes them unique, so that they are recognizable without being stereotypical or predictable.

All of the teen characters are more or less equal, if not in screen time, then in dramatic importance. Each character has his or her own conflict and resolution. The through line of each teen can be summed up as follows:

Brian: Brian's time with the Breakfast Club helps him to separate his parents' goals from his own needs. Through his encounter with Bender, in particular, Brian learns to accept failure as an unavoidable and valuable part of growing up.

Claire: Thanks to the Breakfast Club, ever-popular Claire discovers there is an alternative to the shallow relationships she has with her other friends and her parents. Her unexpected kinship with Brian and Allison helps her to accept the "geek" in herself.

Bender: After sharing the unhappy side of his life with the Breakfast Club, Bender is able to accept comfort from them. Bender discovers that he can show pain and not be rejected. This, in turn, makes him more accepting and sympathetic to others.

Andrew: During detention, Andrew turns away from Claire, the type of girl he normally associates with, toward Allison. Allison's willingness to reveal herself encourages Andrew to come clean about his recent bad behavior. Andrew decides to stop living his father's life and be his own man.

When the characters are first introduced, it might be hard to imagine that Allison (played by Ally Sheedy, above) and Andrew would have much in common. The bond the two come to share highlights the characters' development.

Allison: Like Bender, terrified Allison learns the value of sharing and trusting. Opening up allows her to express her attraction to Andrew.

PROTAGONIST VS. ANTAGONIST

As the teacher in charge of detention, Vernon opposes the students and creates a series of obstacles for them. He is not a villain in the traditional sense, however. Instead, Vernon represents the worst of the adult world—its bigotry, hopelessness, and tyranny. He is more of an institutional force than an individual antagonist, but by belittling and disregarding the students, he motivates them to change.

Over the course of the film, the teens confront Vernon's prejudices, and the assumptions he makes about them. The point of the story, however, is not for the teens to defeat Vernon directly, or to alter his perception of them, but to change how they perceive themselves.

Unlike in *On the Waterfront*, there is no final confrontation between good and bad, protagonist vs. antagonist. Instead, Brian leaves behind a pointed essay, declaring the teens's victory over Vernon's defeatism. As is the case in many nontraditional films, the conflict in *The Breakfast Club* is as much a battle within the characters as between them.

Supporting Characters

The most visible supporting character in *The Breakfast Club* is Carl, the janitor. A former all-star student at the high school, Carl functions as Vernon's sounding board. Carl humanizes the teacher, first by scolding him for snooping in the confidential personnel files and then by questioning his callous attitudes.

> VERNON
> What did you want to be when you were young?

> CARL
> When I was a kid, I wanted to be John Lennon.

> VERNON
> Carl don't be a goof! I'm trying to make a serious point here . . . I've been teaching for twenty-two years, and each year . . . these kids get more and more arrogant.

> CARL
> . . . Come on Vern, the kids haven't changed, you have! You took a teaching position, 'cause you thought it'd be fun, right? Thought you could have summer vacations off . . . and then you found out it was actually work . . . and that really bummed you out.

> VERNON
>
> These kids turned on me . . .

> CARL
>
> Come on. Listen Vern, if you were sixteen, what would you think of you, huh?

> VERNON
>
> Hey . . . Carl, you think I [really care] what these kids think of me?

> CARL
>
> Yes, I do . . .[6]

Although they have very little screen time, the teens' parents also play a significant role as supporting characters. They are the students' offscreen foils. Like Vernon, they are forces with which the teens must wrestle in order to change and mature.

Dialogue

In *On the Waterfront*, much of the characters' speech is differentiated by their age and level of education. In *The Breakfast Club*, Hughes uses his characters' social position to distinguish their voices. The teens are more or less the same age, but they come from different backgrounds and have different interests.

The following exchange, which takes place in the library, points out the characters' differences. Bored

and angry, Bender rips pages out of a book and throws them around.

> ANDREW
> That's real intelligent.

> BENDER
> You're right. It's wrong to destroy literature.

> BENDER
> It's such fun to read . . . and, Molet really [thrills me]!

COMEDY OR DRAMA?

The Breakfast Club is a comedy-drama. Comedy-dramas blend humor and drama, but their overall thrust is more serious than comic. Often they begin on a light, comic note and turn darker as the piece goes on. In other cases, however, the two sides co-mingle throughout.

Examples of recent movie dramedies include *About a Boy* (2002), *About Schmidt* (2002), *Lost in Translation* (2003), and *Sideways* (2004). Television dramedies include *Las Vegas*, *Grey's Anatomy*, and *Desperate Housewives*.

CLAIRE

Mol-yare.

BRIAN

I love his work.[7]

As this excerpt shows, Bender peppers his speech with sarcasm and aggressive language, but he cannot pronounce the French name Molière correctly. Claire and Brian, on the other hand, not only pronounce Molière correctly, but let the others know they are familiar with his plays.

The Breakfast Club is filled with this type of exchange. Words are the teens' weapons of choice. They use them to attack one another, as well as to deflect and hide. In the following exchange, Andrew responds to Allison's question about why he received detention:

ANDREW

I'm here today because uh, because my coach and my father don't want me to blow my ride. See, I get treated differently because uh, Coach thinks I'm a winner. So does my old man. I'm not a winner because I wannabe one. . . I'm a winner because I got strength and speed. Kinda like a racehorse. That's about how involved I am in what's happening to me.

91

>   ALLISON
> Yeah? That's very interesting. Now
> why don't you tell me why you're
> really in here.
>
>   ANDREW
> Forget it![8]

Hughes uses the interrogation technique to great effect in *The Breakfast Club*. Many questions are posed, but only a choice few are answered.

WRITING FOR TELEVISION

Narrative television (as opposed to reality, educational, or news shows) is divided into four major types: miniseries; two-hour movies-of-the-week; episodic hour-long dramatic; and episodic thirty-minute sitcom (situation comedy). For the most part, narrative television writing follows the same basic rules as movie writing. A movie-of-the-week script looks a lot like a feature film script. All the genres used in moviemaking are also used in television. There are, however, a few significant differences between the two.

PREMISE

Like movies, TV shows have premises. Episodic TV shows actually have two premises—the series premise, and the premise of individual episodes. Some series are self-contained—that is, each episode begins with a fresh story and has a definite ending. *Law & Order* and *CSI: Crime Scene Investigation* are examples of series that are self-contained. Although the same main characters appear every week, a new set of crimes is investigated with each episode. Other series, like *Lost*, *Gilmore Girls*, *7th Heaven*, and *The O.C.*, are open-ended. Their story lines develop over an entire season or more.

In self-contained shows, the premise is clear and finite. The series premise of *CSI*, for instance, is "determination leads to victory." The determination of the forensic detectives to solve the mystery leads to the capture of the criminals. The premises of open-ended series, however, tend to be more thematic than dramatic. The theme of *Lost* is rebirth, or starting over, while self-discovery defines *Gilmore Girls*.

According to creator-writer Yvette Lee-Bowser, her 1990s sitcom *Living Single* had a different theme for each season: "Each pre-season we sit down and talk about what the evolution of character is going to be. We try to come up with a theme for the season that will give us some story ideas along the way"[1] One season of *Living Single* focused on reaching for one's dreams, while another was about self-empowerment.

When putting together an open-ended TV series, creators usually plan an entire season's worth of story lines at a time, with individual episodes functioning as a sequence within the bigger story. Each episode nonetheless stands on its own and tells a complete story.

BIBLES

All TV series have "bibles," a set of rules that govern the world of the show. Bibles are produced by the show's creators, those writers who come up with the original idea for the series. A series bible details how the show is set up—open or closed, solo, duo or ensemble leads—and its premise. It includes all of the show's recurring characters, their histories, and how they interact with one another.

The bible also describes the show's setting, its locales and time period, and any recurring storytelling devices. For example, the first season of *Lost* used flashbacks to reveal relevant information about the plane crash survivors. The *Lost* bible notes the flashbacks and how they are woven into the present-day story. Another device of the show involves the passage of time. Some of the episodes begin at the same point in time, but are told from different characters' perspectives. This device is also noted in the series bible.

SUBPREMISES

Most of the time, a single episode of a series will contain multiple story lines and subpremises. Thirty minute shows typically have two or three subpremises. Within an hour-long episode, there may be as many as eight separate story lines, each with its own subpremise, although two to four story lines is more common.

Jorge Garcia, Matthew Fox, Daniel Roebuck, Evangeline Lilly, Mira Furlan, and Terry O'Quinn (left to right), in a scene from the first season of Lost.

Starting with the main, or "A" plot, story lines are then broken down by the amount of screen time each one gets. The "A" story will be slightly longer than the "B" story, the "B" story longer than the "C" story, and so forth.

TV writers usually organize subpremises around a single theme, which changes from week to week. The theme of a single episode of *7th Heaven*, for example, might be self-sacrifice or forgiveness. All of the story lines dramatize the chosen theme in some way and interconnect with one another. One of the plots might be comic, while the others are serious.

STRUCTURE

Although television structure mimics movie structure in many ways, it differs in one big way—commercial breaks. The action must come to a complete halt every ten minutes or so. Because of those breaks, television writers conceive their scripts in short, definite acts. An hour-long show typically contains four acts, including an act-one teaser. Thirty-minute sitcoms have two acts, with a teaser.

> TEASER—A brief scene designed to hook a viewer into continuing to watch a show.

Teasers take place in the first few pages of the script and are designed to keep the audience from switching shows during the first commercial break. While one-hour teasers introduce the audience to that week's conflict, sitcom teasers rarely do. In sitcoms, teasers merely set the joke-telling mood, without revealing much about the story to come.

Each act of a television show has its own beginning, middle, and end—its own conflict, rising action, and conclusion. Some shows end each episode on cliffhangers. Similar to teasers, cliffhangers leave the viewer "dangling," curious about what will happen to the characters the following week. The characters may be left in actual danger or in a state of emotional turmoil.

CHARACTERS

In addition to open and closed plot categories, TV series can be divided into three types based on character. As the name implies, solo lead character shows revolve around the activities of one main character. *House* and *The New Adventures of Old Christine* are examples of single-character shows. Although *House* and *Christine* may be surrounded by helpers and family members, they are always the primary focus of their shows.

Duo lead character shows, like *Gilmore Girls* and *Two and a Half Men*, divide the focus evenly between two main characters. Ensemble shows have large, diverse casts, though one character may function as leader and have slightly more screen time than the others. When the premise of a show revolves around a place, such as a hospital, police station, office, or apartment building, the cast is frequently an ensemble. Crime and medical dramas,

William Petersen and Jorja Fox in a scene from the 2005–06 season of C.S.I.: Crime Scene Investigation.

like *ER*, *CSI*, and *Law & Order*, usually fall into the ensemble category.

Although ensemble shows, by definition, have no lead characters, individual episodes often do. Writers will select one character to put in the "A" story line one week, then another character the following week. For example, in one episode of *ER*, Dr. Weaver's search for her biological mother might be the "A" story line, while the next episode might highlight Dr. Kovak's budding romance with nurse Sam. Dr. Weaver will have more screen time in episode one, but less in episode two.

DIALOGUE

Since TV depends heavily on dialogue, writers take extra care to create consistent voices for their characters. Sitcom dialogue is highly stylized, as characters deliver one-liners at a regular clip. If the character is developed around a specific actor, as in *Seinfeld*, the dialogue will reflect that actor's particular speaking style.

In addition, shows themselves might have their own recognizable style of dialogue. *ER* and *West Wing* became famous for their dialogue-on-the-run style. While moving from room to room, characters carry on rapid-fire conversations. The viewer gets the gist of what is being said, but not all the words. In the *CSI* shows, on the other hand, the forensics detectives carefully explain procedures as they are doing them. The on-the-run dialogue style makes

Rachel Bilson, Mischa Barton, Adam Brody, and Benjamin McKenzie (left to right), from the 2005–06 season of The O.C., are an example of an ensemble cast.

viewers feel as though they are peeking in on the world of the show. The *CSI* style, on the other hand, brings the audience right into the world.

To create a believable setting for the weekly viewer, medical and legal series often use technical language in their dialogue. The following excerpt from an episode of *ER* exemplifies that series' fast-paced, specialized dialogue. In it, doctors and nurses are working on an unconscious gunshot victim just rushed into the emergency room:

> HALEH
>
> BP's down, 80/40.

> LEWIS
>
> Let's get a CBC, chem seven, type and cross two units.

> HICKS
>
> Order a chest film and do a CT on the way to ICU.

> GREENE
>
> Pupils are blown.

> LEWIS
>
> No reflexes, flaccid paralysis.

> HICKS
>
> Let's get a gas.

TEAM TV

In television, writers are the most important players in the creative process. Unlike in feature film writing, television writing is done in teams, led by the show's creators. Every series employs a staff of experienced writers. Some also hire outside writers to work on a particular episode.

Television series operate on a tight production schedule, and writers typically have less time to create their scripts than feature film writers. Sitcoms, most of which are shot on a soundstage before a live audience, are rewritten and finalized over the course of a week. Writer Yvette Lee-Bowser described a typical workweek on the sitcom *Living Single*: "On Thursday morning we will read a script. On Thursday afternoon we see a run-through. We do rewrites on that script based on what did or didn't work on its feet. On Friday we see the show again on stage. The network and the studios give us their notes and we do a rewrite based on that. On Monday, the staff is basically polishing a script that is coming up in the future."[2]

                    MALIK
          You want me to track down her
          family?

                    GREENE
          Yeah. And Haleh, check her wallet.
          Maybe there's a donor card on her
          driver's license.

                    LEWIS
          Yeah, that's likely.[3]

Viewers do not need to understand the specifics of what the actors are saying in this scene, as long as the dialogue sounds credible for the characters. The short lines spoken by five different characters set a quick tempo, and the mixture of impersonal medical jargon and sarcasm and concern hints at the show's overall tone.

A CAREER IN SCREENWRITING

P ursuing a career in screenwriting can be a difficult task. It requires talent and passion, as well as tremendous commitment and a thick skin. Very few succeed. If the desire and perseverance are there, however, writing for the screen can be financially and artistically rewarding.

The most important tool for a screenwriting career is knowledge—knowledge of the craft of screenwriting and knowledge of the world. Accomplished screenwriters are curious about life around them and what makes people tick. They read books and magazines, look at art, listen to music, go to the theater, and keep up with current events.

They also watch a lot of movies and television. When they watch movies, however, they break them down and study them. They try to understand what makes them succeed or fail. Beginning screenwriters can benefit from not only watching the great movies of the past, but also by reading scripts by the best writers. Some have been published in book form; others are available on the Internet.

Each type of script is different: a transcript of a finished film, with dialogue and sparse stage direction; a last draft of a preproduction script; or a shooting script. Early drafts of a screenplay are the most useful for study purposes, because they best reflect the writer's intentions. They tend to be fuller and richer than shooting scripts and transcriptions.

Below is a list of films with notable screenplays, many of which have been published in book form. Some, like *Chinatown*, *Some Like It Hot*, and *Shakespeare in Love*, are remarkable for their dialogue. Others, like *The Sixth Sense* and *All About Eve,* are notable for their structure. Still others, like *The Godfather*, *Citizen Kane*, and *The Seven Samurai*, stand out for their range and scope. All have exceptionally well-drawn characters.

1. *All About Eve* by Joseph Mankiewicz (1950)
2. *Bonnie and Clyde* by David Newman and Robert Benton (1967)
3. *Citizen Kane* by Herman Mankiewicz and Orson Welles (1941)
4. *Casablanca* by Julius J. Epstein, Philip G. Epstein, and Howard Koch (1942)
5. *Chinatown* by Robert Towne (1974)
6. *Dog Day Afternoon* by Frank Pierson (1975)

106

A career in writing can be difficult, with a great deal of work re-writing material often required.

7. *The Godfather* by Mario Puzo and Francis Ford Coppola (1972)

8. *It's a Wonderful Life* by Francis Goodrich, Albert Hackett, and Frank Capra (1946)

9. *One Flew Over the Cuckoo's Nest* (1975) by Bo Goldman and Lawrence Hauben

10. *Rain Man* by Ronald Bass and Barry Morrow (1988)

11. *The Seven Samurai* by Akria Kurosawa, Shinobu Hashimoto, and Hideo Oguni (1954)

12. *Shakespeare in Love* by Marc Norman and Tom Stoppard (1998)

13. *The Sixth Sense* by M. Night Shyamalan (1999)

14. *Some Like It Hot* by Billy Wilder and I. A. L. Diamond (1959)

15. *Stagecoach* by Dudley Nichols (1939)

16. *Taxi Driver* by Paul Schrader (1976)

17. *To Kill a Mockingbird* by Horton Foote (1962)

18. *Tootsie* by Larry Gelbart and Murray Schisgal (1982)

ADVICE FROM THE EXPERTS

What inspires screenwriters? Anything and everything. Real-life experiences, dreams, songs, paintings, magazine articles, history books, fiction—all can be sources of inspiration. No two writers work in the same way. Some need the discipline of routine—nine-to-five, five days a week, or ten pages every day. Others prefer a more spontaneous approach. Some outline their stories in detail, compiling scene-by-scene breakdowns on note cards. Others start with a beginning and an end and go from there.

Over the years, many experienced screenwriters have offered advice on how to get started writing for the movies and television. Below are observations and suggestions from a few writers who made it.

Diane Frolov (*The Chris Isaak Show*) advises: "read as much as you possibly can and do many different things. I'm always interested in writers who bring something else into the writing than just film school and just having watched TV."[1]

Fay Kanin (*Heartsounds*) offers this: "My advice is to write what you like, to please yourself, and then to be a bulldog about trying to get it made. Don't give up."[2]

Amy Holden Jones (*Beethoven*, *Indecent Proposal*) says: "stay within a genre for your first couple of scripts. Study it, learn about it. . . . Go to a library that has scripts, and study the classic scripts of that genre you've chosen. . . . Reading a script is not the same as seeing a movie. You have to read the script. It also starts you off aspiring to the best."[3]

Marc Norman (*Shakespeare in Love*) says: "The way to have a real career as a [screen]writer is to hire yourself out. . . . But when you do hire yourself out, the thing you have to remember is that you

Screenwriter Akiva Goldsman has a conversation with actor Paul Bettany on the set of the film The Da Vinci Code *in early 2006.*

better put some passion on the page. These guys who hire you are renting your passion."[4]

Eric Daniel, who participated in the Disney Fellowship Program and worked as an assistant for filmmaker Spike Lee, encourages aspiring writers to learn everything they can about movie production. He also advises young writers to "know how to accept feedback and reaction to your work, and you have to know how to deal with it and utilize it to improve your work."[5]

VIDEO ON THE WEB

The World Wide Web has proven to be an excellent outlet for filmmakers who are just starting out. Sites such as YouTube, Google video, Yahoo! video, and iFilm allow their users to put their original videos on display for the whole world to see. These and other websites have spawned the phenomenon of "viral video"—which is what happens when a video file is emailed/ shared with friends, who in turn forward the video to their other friends, who forward it to still other friends, and so on. This is a quick and easy way to reach the public with your film, but getting your work noticed could be difficult. YouTube, for example, had 9 million unique visitors to its site in February 2006, and was showing more than 40 million videos a day at that time.[6]

SCHOOLS AND UNIVERSITIES

Although a college degree in screenwriting is not a requirement for employment in the industry, having some formal education helps. Screenwriting requires creativity, analysis, and self-discipline. Courses in screenwriting encourage students to write on a schedule, and they provide valuable feedback from teachers and fellow students. In addition, many schools allow student scripts to be performed by actors or to be made into real movies. These hands-on opportunities can be an invaluable learning tool.

According to a 2005 *New York Times* article, more then six hundred colleges and universities in the United States offer programs in film studies or related subjects. Many of these offer degrees in film production, and some even offer specialized degrees in screenwriting. High school graduates can also attend one-year film schools with screenwriting specialties.

Schools with film programs are located not only in California, but across the United States. Below is a partial list of four-year colleges that offer film degrees with screenwriting specialization:

- Bennington College, Bennington, Vermont
- Brigham Young University, Provo, Utah
- Chapman University, Orange, California
- Drexel University, Philadelphia, Pennsylvania
- DePaul University, Chicago, Illinois
- Loyola Marymount University, Los Angeles, California
- New York University, Tisch School of the Arts Dramatic Writing Program, New York, New York
- Metropolitan State University, St. Paul, Minnesota
- Regent University, Virginia Beach, Virginia
- SUNY College at Purchase, Purchase, New York
- University of Michigan, Ann Arbor, Michigan
- University of California, Los Angeles (UCLA), Los Angeles, California

SCREENPLAY FORMAT

Screenplays are written in a specific, recognizable format. Commercial screenwriting software, such as *Final Draft* and *Movie Magic*, is designed to automatically format text as it is typed. *ScriptBuddy*, a free Internet program, allows users to compose properly formatted script text while online.

Using the style sheet function, any computer word processing program, such as Microsoft Word, can be set up to format the parts of a script. Below are a few general guidelines for feature film script formatting:

1. To allow for three-hole punching, the left margin is set at 1.5 inches, the right at 1 inch.
2. Page numbers are placed in the upper right hand corner, 1 inch from right, ½ inch from top.
3. Scene setting indicators, called slug lines, are capitalized. "Interior" and "exterior" are abbreviated as INT. and EXT. Example: INT. LIVING ROOM—DAY
4. Descriptive text (stage directions) is 60 characters, or 6 inches wide, flush left and single-spaced.
5. Character names are capitalized and centered.
6. Parenthetical text, called wrylies, is placed below and one or two tabs to the left of the character name.
7. Dialogue is indented and is 35 characters, or 3.5 inches wide.
8. Lines of continuous dialogue and lines of continuous stage direction are single-spaced. Double-spacing is used between a block of dialogue and stage directions.

- University of Southern California, Los Angeles, California

The following community colleges offer two-year degrees in screenwriting:
- Minneapolis Community and Technical College, Minneapolis, Minnesota
- Scottsdale Community College, Scottsdale, Arizona

The New York Film Academy, which has branches in New York City, Los Angeles, and London, has a one-year diploma program in screenwriting. The Academy also offers a special summer program for high school students.

WRITING CONTESTS

The writing world offers dozens of screenwriting contests. Most are geared toward adult (over 21) writers, but a few, listed below, aim specifically for younger contestants.

REELtalent Film Festival Screenwriting Competition
Sponsor: Young Filmmakers Society
Mission: To educate and promote young filmmakers
Eligibility: 21 or younger
http://www.young-filmmakers.org
P. O. Box 336
Chappaqua, New York 10514

The Studio Academy Screenwriting Contest
Sponsor: The Studio Academy

SCREENWRITER SALARIES

Starting Salary	Experienced Salary	Star Salary
As low as $20,000	Up to $100,000	Millions (?)

Salaries for film/TV jobs are very elusive, as it is usually freelance work and you are often selling a product (your script) as opposed to being hired by an employer. Unless you are part of the writing staff for a television series, payment can be very sporadic. (And even on a TV series, income is lost when a show goes on hiatus or if it is cancelled.)

An original union screenplay can sell for as low as $20,000 up to the millions. Nonunion productions might not pay anything up front, but promise the writer a cut of the box office. A writer can make a lot in one year, but nothing for years afterward. The salary of a "working screenwriter" is supposedly between $20,000 to $100,000 a year, but again, there may be years when the writer makes nothing.

Mission: To open doors to unknown writers
throughout the country
Eligibility: 12 to adult
http://www.thestudioacademy.org

Screen Teens Scriptwriting Contest for Youth
Under 21
Sponsor: On Cue Productions
http://fade.to/screenteens
P. O. Box 96097
Yreka, California 96097

CHAPTER NOTES

INTRODUCTION

1. Studs Turkel, ed., *American Dreams, Lost and Found* (New York: Pantheon, 1980), pp. 56–57.

CHAPTER 1. ELEMENTS OF SCREENWRITING: PREMISE, SENSORY STYLE, AND STRUCTURE

1. Joel Engel, ed., *Oscar-Winning Screenwriters on Screenwriting* (New York: Hyperion, 2002), p. 140.

2. Lajos Egri, *The Art of Dramatic Writing* (New York: Simon and Schuster, 1960), pp. 1, 6.

3. Lorian Tamara Elberg, ed., *Why We Write: Personal Statements and Photographic Portraits of 25 Top Screenwriters* (Los Angeles, California: Silman-James Press, 1999), p. 61.

4. Ibid., pp. 61–62.

5. Ibid., p. 45.

6. Engel, p. 22.

7. Ibid., p. 23.

8. Frances Goodrich, Albert Hackett, and Frank Capra, *It's a Wonderful Life* (Monterey Park, California: O.S.P. Publishing, 1994), p. 89.

9. Paul Schrader, *Taxi Driver* (London: Faber and Faber, 1990), p. 26.

10. Engel, p. 123.

11. Joel Engel, ed., *Screenwriters on Screenwriting* (New York: Hyperion, 2002), p. 170.

CHAPTER 2. ELEMENTS OF SCREENWRITING: CHARACTERS AND DIALOGUE

1. Engel, *Oscar-Writing Screenwriters on Screenwriting* (New York: Hyperion, 2002), p. 172.

2. Lajos Egri, *The Art of Dramatic Writing* (New York: Simon and Schuster, 1960), p. 106.

3. Ibid., p. 107.

4. Ibid., p. 113.

5. Paul Schrader, *Taxi Driver* (London: Faber and Faber, 1990), p. 3.

CHAPTER 3. PUTTING IT ALL TOGETHER: ON THE WATERFRONT

1. Budd Schulberg, *On the Waterfront: The Final Shooting Script* (Hollywood California: Samuel French, 1980), p. 3.

2. Ibid., p. 13.

4. Ibid., p. 55.

5. Ibid., p. 5.

6. Ibid., pp. 68–69.

7. Ibid., p. 104.

8. Ibid., p. 118.

9. Ibid., p. 140.

10. Ibid., p. 47.

11. Ibid., p. 17.

12. Ibid., pp 61–62.

13. Ibid., p. 145.

14. Ibid., p. 152.

15. Ibid., p. 39.

Chapter 4. Putting It All Together: The Breakfast Club

1. John Hughes, *The Breakfast Club* (Universal Pictures, 1984), p. 1.

2. Ibid.

3. Ibid., p. 66.

4. Ibid., p. 67.

5. Ibid., pp. 81-82.

6. Ibid., pp. 58-59.

7. Ibid., pp. 23.

8. Ibid., p. 33.

Chapter 5. Writing for Television

1. Erich Leon Harris, *African-American Screenwriters Now* (Los Angeles, California: Silman-James Press, 1999), p. 230.

2. Ibid., pp. 236–237.

3. Lydin Woodward, "Motherhood," from *ER* (Warner Bros. Television, 1995), pp. 52–53.

CHAPTER 6. A CAREER IN SCREENWRITING

1. William Froug, *The New Screenwriter Looks at the New Screenwriter* (Los Angeles, California: Silman-James Press, 1991), p. 271.

2. Ibid., p. 351.

3. Joel Engel, ed., *Oscar-Winning Screenwriters on Screenwriting* (New York: Hyperion, 2002), p. 78.

4. Ibid., p. 149.

5. Erich Leon Harris, *African-American Screenwriters Now* (Los Angeles, California: Silman-James Press, 1999), p. 102.

6. Lev Grossman, "How to Get Famous in 30 Seconds," *TIME*, April 24, 2006, p. 66.

GLOSSARY

antagonist—In a fictional work, the character who opposes the protagonist and gives rise to the conflict.

character arc—From beginning to end, the emotional change a character undergoes during a story.

cliffhanger—A situation at the end of an act or episode whose outcome is left suspensefully unanswered.

climax—The part in a script with the greatest emotional tension; the highest point in the rising action, just before the resolution.

colloquial—Characteristic of informal, ordinary conversation.

denouement—The final outcome of a story. Also known as resolution.

dramedy—A narrative genre in which the lines between comedy and drama are blurred.

ensemble—A group of co-equal or supporting players.

exposition—The experiences of a story's characters that take place before the main action, and contribute to the characters' motivations and reactions. Also known as back story.

flashback—A scene from the past that interrupts the ongoing action.

genre—A category or type of story a given film falls into.

linear story—A story that progresses in chronological order.

omniscient—Having complete awareness and knowledge.

organically—In a manner similar to natural growth and organization, not artificial.

point of attack—The point or moment at which a scene begins.

point of view—That aspect of storytelling dealing with who tells the story and how it is told.

premise—The dramatic idea driving the plot of a story.

protagonist—The main character of a narrative; the character who engages the reader's interest and sympathy. Also known as the pivotal character.

rising action—In a script's second act, complications in the action that arise out of the core conflict. Rising action intensifies as it goes along, until it reaches a climax.

slug lines—In a film script, the part that indicates a scene's setting and time.

stage directions—A scriptwriter's written instructions about how the actors and, in some cases, the camera, are to move and behave. Also known as the descriptive text.

stereotype—A simplified image or interpretation that has become standardized within a society or group.

storyline—All of the action of a narrative. Also known as the plot.

subplot—The secondary action of a story, that underscores or supports the main action.

through line—The structure of a film narrative, encompassing the conflict, rising action, and resolution. Also known as the spine.

teaser—A brief scene designed to hook the viewer into watching.

turning point—The moment at the end of a script's second act in which the protagonist makes a critical decision.

voice-over—Dialogue spoken over onscreen action by an offscreen narrator.

wrylies—Directions in dialogue text that suggest how an actor is to deliver a line or lines. Wrylies are written in parentheses, between the character name and the dialogue.

FURTHER READING

General Film Books

Arijon, Daniel. *Grammar of the Film Language.* Los Angeles: Silman-James Press, 1991.

Giannetti, Louis. *Understanding Movies.* 10th ed. Upper Saddle River, N.J.: Prentice Hall, 2005.

Monaco, James. *How to Read a Film: The World of Movies, Media, and Multimedia.* New York: Oxford University Press, 2000.

Peacock, Richard Beck. *The Art of Moviemaking: Script to Screen.* Upper Saddle River, N.J.: Prentice Hall, 2001.

Screenwriting Books

Ebert, Lorian Tamara. *Why We Write: Personal Statements and Photographic Portraits of 25 Top Screenwriters.* Los Angeles: Silman-James Press, 1991.

Engel, Joel. *Oscar-Winning Screenwriters on Screenwriting: The Award-Winning Best in the Business Discuss Their Craft.* New York: Hyperion, 2002.

Engel, Joel. *Screenwriters on Screenwriting*. New York: Hyperion, 1995.

Froug, William. *The New Screenwriter Looks at the New Screenwriter*. Los Angeles: Silman-James Press, 1991.

Grube, G. M. A., translator. *Aristotle: On Poetry and Style*. Indianapolis: The Bobbs-Merrill Company, 1958.

Harris, Erich Leon. *African-American Screenwriters Now*. Los Angeles: Silman-James Press, 1991.

McKee, Robert. *Story: Substance, Structure, Style and the Principles of Screenwriting*. New York: Regan Books, 1997.

Rannow, Jerry. *Writing Television Comedy*. New York: Allworth Press, 1999.

Seger, Linda. *Creating Unforgettable Characters*. New York: H. Holt, 1990.

Seger, Linda. *Making a Good Script Great*. Hollywood: Samuel French, 1994.

Trottier, David. *The Screenwriter's Bible: A Complete Guide to Writing, Formatting, and Selling Your Script*. Los Angeles: Silman-James Press, 1998.

INTERNET ADDRESSES

Screenwriter's Utopia

http://www.screenwritersutopia.com/

Screenplay Archive and Related Discussions

http://www.screenplays-online.de

Writers Guild of America, West

http://www.www.wga.org

YouTube.com

http://www.youtube.com

INDEX